Advance Praise for *Who Says It's a Man...*

"Investing in this book is investing in your future. It's smart and strategic, but savvy and saucy, too."

—Cathie Black, Author of the *New York Times* bestseller *Basic Black: The Essential Guide for Getting Ahead at Work (and in Life)*

"In *Who Says It's a Man's World*, Emily has triggered a new and necessary conversation about how to best activate women's career success—and it's all about starting with a big shift in our perception. Between her illuminating research, probing questions, ferocious wit, inspiring examples, and practical activities, Emily has ensured that women of all ages will have the know-how and a step-by-step pathway to become influencers, or as she says, 'rock stars,' at any stage of our careers."

—Alexia Vernon, Author of *90 Days 90 Ways: Onboard Young Professionals to Peak Performance*

"Unique in chronicling the personal and professional, the outer and the self-imposed, barriers women face. Even better, Emily's expertise equips readers with the strategies we need to rule—not just survive in—today's workplace. A rare and exciting book that reaches deep into the heart of a workplace and discloses not only its day-to-day inner workings, but also the very personal victories, problems, doubts, and joys awaiting its female members."

—Selena Rezvani, Award-winning *Washington Post* columnist on women and leadership, and author of *Pushback: How Smart Women Ask—And Stand Up—For What They Want*

"Emily has hit the nail on the head with sharp, tactical advice for the aspiring CEO in all of us. With a wise (and wry!) perspective, she brings humor and grace to a host of difficult workplace situations."

—Kathryn Minshew, Founder and CEO, The Daily Muse & Company Muse

"Written with keen personal insight and humor (and a mega-dose of reality) this book is a must-read for anyone wanting more success and fulfillment in their corporate career than they are getting—but not knowing why they aren't getting it. Bennington spells out step-by-step how to decisively make progress on your long-term aspirations by what you choose to THINK and DO every single day. She outlines the action steps to get there as clearly as she flags the self-inflicted, career-destroying mistakes many of us make."

—Patty Azzarello, President of the Azzarello Group and author of *Rise: 3 Practical Steps for Advancing Your Career, Standing Out as a Leader,* and *Liking Your Life*

"Emily Bennington has a candid and real way of using anecdotes to draw us in and connect us through shared experiences. For those who prefer the mystery and call of self-reflection, she offers pragmatic and prescriptive tools as well as a good dose of prodding and wit. Amidst the pages, you will find, as I have, many kindred spirits."

—Maria R. Lachapelle, 22-year crisis and
corporate communications executive

"The 'New Economy' is every woman's opportunity to define life and work on her own terms. Thanks to Emily Bennington for reminding us that we are living in a watershed time of professional reinvention and creativity where WE can truly create our own lives."

—Amanda Steinberg, Founder, DailyWorth.com

"A terrific book that explains how to build on all of the wonderful parts of being a woman to achieve any goal we set."

—Cali Williams Yost, CEO and Founder,
Flex + Strategy Group and author of *TWEAK
IT: Make What Matters to You Happen Every Day*

"This is a book with A LOT of uummpph! I love that Emily brings her extensive study of holistic wellness into the boardroom to help women 'tame the mental monkey' and find peace and clarity in the midst of incredibly demanding lives and careers. One for the desk AND the nightstand!"

—Jodi Glickman, Founder of Great on the Job
and author of *Great on the Job: What to Say,
How to Say It — The Secrets of Getting Ahead*

"As a mid-career professional, I found this book to be enlightening both to my own personal path as well as my day-to-day work. I truly believe this is required reading for anyone looking to take charge of their life and career."

—Pamela Ruiz, Director, Family Engagement,
Young Presidents' Organization, Inc.

who says it's a man's world

the girls' guide to corporate domination

EMILY BENNINGTON

HARPERCOLLINS
LEADERSHIP

AN IMPRINT OF HARPERCOLLINS

Who Says It's A Man's World

© 2013 Emily Bennington

Published by HarperCollins Leadership, an imprint of HarperCollins Focus LLC.

Any internet addresses, phone numbers, or company or product information printed in this book are offered as a resource and are not intended in any way to be or to imply an endorsement by HarperCollins Leadership, nor does HarperCollins Leadership vouch for the existence, content, or services of these sites, phone numbers, companies, or products beyond the life of this book.

Bulk discounts available. For details visit:
www.harpercollinsleadership.com/bulkquotes
Email: customercare@harpercollins.com

ISBN 978-1-4002-3106-5 (TP)

Perfectly nice guys will say to me, "You must be so happy you've won." But when I reply, "Are you working for a woman?" they look appalled.

—Gloria Steinem

Dedicated to
iron ladies everywhere.

contents

PART ONE: CUT THE CRAP
Section 1: Self-Awareness

foreword

It is with great pleasure that I get to be the first raving fan to recommend *Who Says It's a Man's World* to all women (and men) as a must-read career guide. Had I read this book before becoming a bona fide "executive," it would have saved me from making a number of behavioral errors that Emily so accurately describes.

In fact, while reading the first part of the book—which focuses on behaviors that cause us to block our own success—I vividly recalled the *numerous* times I found myself in the exact same situations. In some cases, I know my behaviors actually could have—and may have!—set back my career. (Oh, how many of us learn "the hard way" what *not* to do at work!) But that's precisely what makes this book such an invaluable tool for professional women: We no longer have to question ourselves on what the correct behavior is or isn't. Indeed, when I was coming up through the ranks, I would often ask peers who were at the same stage in their careers about the correct protocol for executives. Of course, this was a mistake because they didn't know, either! But peers tend to talk to peers, because we often do not feel comfortable asking our superiors. It's happened to me hundreds of times throughout my career. Now we (both you and I) have a resource to refer to that correctly identifies those core behaviors we should emulate as we navigate the web of corporate life.

Of course, success is more than just knowing the behaviors to avoid, it's also about aligning with the *right* actions, or what I've often referred to as being an "A-player." This is where career books have typically missed the target, in my opinion, by focusing more on the management of others and less about "walking the talk" yourself. But *all* of the great models on leadership that I have observed in my career are about modeling what you preach, which is not new in theory but, ironically, is less emphasized as we move up the ladder.

However, as Emily correctly argues, being a living demonstration to others that you, in fact, believe your own message is—truly—the best way to have impact at work, and it's where we should spend the *most* time. That said, as women, we often emulate what we have seen in our male counterparts as they attend to massive paperwork on their massive desks—when we should do just the opposite! We should get out from behind our desks and be with our teams, showing them through our behaviors what real "professionalism" looks like. (If you're wondering what that is, you must read this book!)

Who Says It's a Man's World is a jewel of a book, and I would recommend it to every professional—both current and aspiring. I know you will benefit from the hundreds of bits of wisdom as I have and even chuckle a lot, too—as I did.

—Ann Rhoades
  Founding Executive, JetBlue Airways

acknowledgments

Three years ago I opened a new doc on my computer, called it *New Girlz Club*, and then stared at the blinking cursor, paralyzed, for well over an hour. From that day to this one, 10 titles and 200 pages later, has been quite a ride, let me tell you. So it is with deep gratitude that I acknowledge those who have been with me throughout this journey, and whose continued support enables me to live my dream each day.

To **Ann Rhoades**, for the exceptional Foreword and for being a true leader in values-driven business. I wish everyone "got it" the way you do.

To my amazing agent **Linda Konner**, for always being on my side. You are simply *the best*, and I look forward to many more collaborations!

To my editor and fellow Anglophile **Ellen Kadin**, who probably got into publishing for a love of the written word but then found herself working with authors like moi. Thank you for making me dust off my fierce stilettos and for giving me a chance, and then another chance, to write this book.

To **Jenny Wesselmann Schwartz**—"Queen of the Catalog"—who swooped in at the 11th hour with the title that saved the day. A million thank-yous.

To **Cathleen Ouderkirk**, for the retro book cover and extra searching for just the right spike.

To my *Effective Immediately* coauthor, dear friend, and mentor **Skip Lineberg**. If every boss grew women leaders like you, there would be no need for this book.

To **Tory Johnson**, for making me walk on fire—literally—and for believing in me when it counted.

To **Kate Betts**, the first executive woman I ever knew—albeit from the TV screen and mastheads of *Vogue* and *Harper's Bazaar*—until the magic of Twitter brought us together.

To **Patti Johnson** and everyone at PeopleResults who prove that great kindness and great margins can and do coexist. (Patti, let's "start the wave" on that one!)

To **Jan Fields, Valarie Gelb, Liz Lange, Ingrid Vanderveldt, Arie Ball, Julie Smolyansky, Dani Ticktin Koplik, Heather Bresch, Susan Bulkeley Butler**, and **Ingrid Ciprian-Matthews** for sharing your stories, and to everyone who contributed to the survey research for this book.

To the big brains at *Forbes Woman*, especially maestro **Caroline Howard**, for keeping the gender debate lively and for giving me the opportunity to connect with so many women I love.

To my family, especially my dad, **Paul Bennington**, who has no idea how much being a latchkey kid prepared me to be an independent adult.

To my husband, **Johnny Tugwell**, who reminds me every day why the first step to "having it all" is marrying a true partner, and for showing me what it really means to lead by example.

To my munchkins, **Christian** and **Liam,** who are already showing a profound appreciation for strong women.

And to my divine spiritual teachers, who took me from a human *do*ing to a human *be*ing, the greatest career lesson of all.

ding, dong!
the bitch is dead

A FEW YEARS ago I worked for a corporate public account-ing firm that hired a whip-smart new grad named Asha.

While our firm was among the 15th largest in the country, many top recruits heard the siren call of even bigger companies and Asha—being a star student—had her choice of any of them. I knew she had recently wrapped up an internship with a partic-ular big firm-that-shall-remain-nameless and received an employment offer, too. So, over a cold beer at a baseball game we sponsored (ah, corporate life) I asked her why she chose us.

"The people."

She answered without hesitation—and I knew what she meant. While still being very corporate—right down to the boring gray walls and penalty fines for missing timesheet deadlines—our firm did make gallant efforts to marry high profits with the hospitality of its Southern roots.

For Asha, the culture-first approach to choosing her employer stemmed from a negative experience she had while interning for the firm-that-shall-remain-nameless. She spoke indignantly about how the company actively encouraged interns to compete with each other by announcing, for example, that only a fraction of those who survived the "three-month job interview" would be brought on full-time. Naturally, this caused the workplace equivalent of bum-rushing lifeboats on the *Titanic*. In one incident, an intern received a last-minute invitation to a reception where firm partners and clients would be in attendance. Sensing a huge opportunity (a.k.a. fish-in-a-barrel networking), the intern kept the event a secret from everyone else and went solo.

If that story makes you go *"Whoa! What a dick!"* you're in the right place.

Because, given the title of this book, *Who Says It's a Man's World*, you may think this is another *go get 'em tigress* guide for women in pencil skirts who would do the same thing while simultaneously ripping a box of copy paper in half with their bare teeth. In fact, maybe you even semi-expect me to say that nice equals weak, emoticons are for losers, and a "survival of the fittest" attitude is the way to get ahead.

Well . . . sorry.

This stereotype of the take-no-prisoners alpha-femme—while promoted gleefully and relentlessly in the media—

makes for great entertainment, but it is deadly to your career in practice. I learned this firsthand at the entry level when I modeled behaviors I thought were "corporate"—only to fall flat on my face. (Think *Devil Wears Prada* ice queen except, sadly, without the Prada.) I remember walking out of my first-ever performance review—crushed—when my boss at the time (and future *Effective Immediately* coauthor) Skip Lineberg told me that I had potential, but virtually no respect from the team. Ouuuuuuuch.

Of course, being a total doormat isn't all that effective either, so the million-dollar question is:

"What does it take for women to win at the highest levels of business?"

Judging by the minuscule number of women who have actually reached such levels, it sometimes feels like the answer is tucked away—Da Vinci Code–style—in a locked box under three feet of marble in an undisclosed location. Women make up half of the workforce and yet, the higher you go up the ladder, the more that number seems to drop . . . and drop. (*Forbes* once called this disparity the *"biggest disappearing act on earth."*) In fact, as I write, women account for just 4 percent of Fortune 500 CEOs, 6 percent of top earners, and 16 percent of board directors and corporate officers. This is a shame for women *and* the bottom line, because when ladies are at the table there's no denying it's good for business. That's not just ra-ra-girl-power talk, by the way. Countless studies have confirmed it, including a five-year analysis of 524 public companies by the research firm Catalyst, which found that organizations with the most women board members outperformed those with the least number of women holding board seats by 16 percent.

Still, after sifting through mountains of data on the business case for gender balance, I wanted to put my own ear to the ground to find out what, specifically, is holding us back and what is propelling us forward. As such, I've spent the last few years surveying more than 700 executive women, interviewing scores of super-achievers for *Forbes*, presenting at numerous women's leadership events, and coaching countless professionals. This was obviously a complex undertaking, so it may surprise you that my conclusion to all this research can be boiled down into one simple sentence.

You must be a magnificent woman *first* to have a magnificent career.

I know, I know. Sounds too simple, right? Like everyone else, you've probably been going about things the other way around—that is, laser-focused on the *job* and what you need to *do* to get ahead. That's important, of course (and covered here), but more than just offering advice on the *what*, this journey is also about digging deep to help you figure out the *who*. In other words, before you can decide what to do in your career, it's important to understand the kind of professional you want to be.

As you'll see in the Woman 2 Woman narratives, the most successful women I've interviewed—McDonald's USA President Jan Fields and Mylan CEO Heather Bresch, among others—all express this need for self-awareness, and by the end of this book you'll be clear on it, too.

You'll know, specifically, the attitudes and behaviors you need to kick to the curb and the ones you need to kick into gear. You'll also have the opportunity to identify your personal core values and apply them to five key professional development areas—self-awareness, social skills, personal effectiveness, team development, and leadership.

This ain't guesswork, people.

The origin of the personal values template is straight from one of the most accomplished people in American history—Ben Franklin—and the career plan template is similar to those used within large, multinational companies and developed in consultation with HR executives serving the Fortune 100.

As you work through this book, and in effect develop your own career path, my hope is that you'll truly understand that "corporate domination" isn't about kicking the door down as so many of us have been (mis)led to believe. (Seriously, save your stilettos.) It's about melting it down one thought, one interaction, and one person at a time. Asha was right. Business is a game about people and—like everything else in life—it all starts with you.

To your magnificence!

@EmilyBennington

P.S. For additional inspiration along your career journey, visit me at www.emilybennington.com.

You Crafty Career Planner, You: How to Use This Book

Who Says It's a Man's World is divided into three parts.

Part One, "Cut the Crap," focuses on behaviors that anyone (both men and women) must ditch to truly be considered professional. These are the most common and insidious roadblocks to success, or what are unaffectionately referred to as "career-killers."

Part Two, "Call in the Good Stuff," is based on the universal law of attraction. In other words, whatever energy you put out in the world is the energy that comes back to you. In the sections here, you're going to get super-clear on what matters most so that you can bring your *whole*, ridiculously positive self to work each day—and teach others how to do the same.

Part Three, "Align with What Works," is designed to help you walk in step with the core competencies of leadership. This is the part where I'll outline, specifically, how you can have influence on the job regardless of whether you have authority (yet!).

Now, here's the equation that ties it all together:

You + 15 Goals + 60 days = Rock Star

If you're ready to get serious and create a roadmap for your success, I have a challenge for you. At the end of each of the first five sections in this book you'll find an Action Plan and a list of professional development goals, each with an assigned point value based on level of difficulty. Your mission is to select three goals from these five sections (that's 15 goals total, for English majors like me who need help with math) and get 'em done in the next 60 days. Roughly, this will shake out to about two goals and two to four hours of time per week over the next two months.

What's that? You want to read the book without creating the plan?

That's a little like hoping your thighs will shrink because you've got a gym membership. It's not the same as actually doing the work. Remember: *No one will ever care about your career—or your thighs—more than you do.* So don't just "kinda" take ownership of what you want. Kinda is for people who will inevitably look back and wonder why they never achieved more. In other words, kinda sucks. But . . . if you're ready to nix kinda and go all in, here's what you do:

1. Start by reading this book in its entirety first. That way you'll have a 10,000-foot view of the whole picture as you pull your career plan together.

2. Select three goals from the end of sections one through five that are most relevant to your career and handwrite them in the career plan template provided in Section 6, i.e., the Toolbox. (Note: If you're thinking *"What's handwriting?"* you can download the e-version at www.emilybennington.com/templates.)

3. Once your goals are in place, check in with yourself regularly, crossing off items you've accomplished and rotating the others into your schedule as needed. When the 60 days are up, simply tally your points to assess your "promotability" on the following scale:

Total Points	Promotability
225 and above	**Rock Star** *(Yeah!)*
150–224	**Backup Band** *(Meh)*
75–149	**Groupie** *(Ewww)*
74 and under	**Nosebleed Seats** *(Sigh . . .)*

You with me?

Good.

Let's roll. . . .

part one
cut the crap

Before we dive into learning new things, let's start by unlearning a few old things, shall we?

Section 1:
SELF-AWARENESS

1	2	3	4	5
Self-Awareness	Social Skills	Personal Effectiveness	Team Development	Leadership
↑ You are here.				

Core Principle

You take full responsibility for your own mind, body, and career with a *daily* practice focused on the process of continued growth and improvement.

In this section, you will learn how to:

- "Catch and release" negative thought patterns.

- Sit still. *Be* still.

- Prevent your kid(s) from competing with your career.

- Mindfully manage stress.

What Your Coworkers Are Thinking

"There's something *different about Amanda."*

CHAPTER ONE

getting rid of the "hob" on your brain

Learning to take responsibility for the nature of our thoughts is the most powerful way to take responsibility for our lives.

—Marianne Williamson

AMBITION GAP, schmambition gap.

Women aren't 16 percent of board directors and corporate officers because the other 84 percent don't want the job. Obviously, there's something else going on.

Glass ceiling, you say?

In some cases perhaps, but in others . . . well, we're simply holding ourselves back. Because as much as we all like to wear our best corporate armor at work (*"I'm a pit bull in lipstick, bitches!*"), the truth is that a lot of us hit an inner glass ceiling long before we ever approach an outer one.

So let's start with that.

For example, let's say you have a colleague who doesn't respond to your e-mail. Instead of thinking, *"Hmmm. Maybe she's slammed,"* does your mind automatically leap to, *"Hmmm. Maybe she's mad at me"*?

Or, what if you have one of those coveted elevator run-ins with your boss's boss? Do you secretly scrutinize every minor word choice—*"Gah! Why did I say that?"*—for the rest of the day?

If so, you've got a hob on the brain.

In folklore, the hob (short for hobgoblin) is a grotesque little creature that exists for the sole purpose of making trouble for human beings. In our world, the hob is that annoying inner critic who always seems to find merciless new ways to say, *"Here's why you suck."* Now, of course there are a million different reasons to wrestle your hob into submission but, for our purposes, this is the biggie:

Bold *thinking* always precedes bold *doing*.

Huge career (and salary!) leaps don't come from waiting until your performance review to be handed incremental bread crumbs. That's lame. They come from knowing your value, going after what you want, and bulldozing through any mental blocks along the way.

Yes, I know it isn't easy, but it *can* be. Truth! There's only one step between you and total freedom (a.k.a. complete hob annihilation) and it's beyond simple. All you have to do is understand—*to the core*—that your inner critic isn't real.

Seriously, it's nothing more than a crotchety, unwelcome houseguest in your head who never leaves. The "hob" has no power whatsoever, so don't give it any. Whenever you have a negative thought pop up—*"I'm never going to get this done"*— take a split second to acknowledge it—*"Thank you for sharing"*— then recast the thought into more productive phrasing—*"I need to break this project down into smaller pieces."* Get it? Initially, you will have to do this—quite literally—moment by moment and thought by thought, but eventually your brain will get with the (re)program. Think about it this way: You are training your mind like you train your muscles. Sure, it hurts at first, but that's how you get stronger.

The Three Biggest Career-Killing Hobs and How to Handle Them

Okay, we all know there's some pretty appalling crap going on in offices today. (And, no, I'm not just referring to those white-collar jailbirds and the need for corporate bailouts.) I'm talking about petty nonsense that—left unchecked—can derail your career faster than you can say, "Double-wide Cubeville4Life."

Of course, your little trickster upstairs loves this stuff—but don't be fooled. All of the behaviors I'm about to describe are muddy career sludge, and the moment you step in any of it will be the moment you stop . . . in . . . your . . . pointy . . . toed . . . tracks.

CAREER-KILLER #1: NEGATIVITY BIAS

While a vigilant threat-and-danger watch was certainly a requirement back when we lived in caves and wore fig leaves, these days it just sucks the oxygen out of the room. Seriously—

who are the people at work you'd hang with even if you weren't paid? Are they the ones who see the cloud in every silver lining? I doubt it. So, if you don't want to be around negative Nancys, chances are your colleagues don't, either.

How to Recognize the Negativity Goblin. When presented with a new idea, does your mind automatically jump to all of the reasons it won't work? If your first and loudest thoughts are always the ones that say *"This is unrealistic," "We've already tried that,"* or *"It'll never happen,"* that's your hob talking.

Take Action. Before you enter a meeting with colleagues, think for a moment about the most annoying person you've ever met. Not someone mean, per se, just someone with mosquito-like qualities (and by that I mean pesky in a way that makes you want to slap 'em). Now, try imagining this person as the voice of your inner critic. Then, when a negative thought like *"We've tried that already"* pops up in your mind, it will be easier to dismiss.

CAREER-KILLER #2: GRUDGES

A few years ago I was in a meeting listening to one of my colleagues over the mothership (a.k.a. that oversize orb planted in the middle of boardroom tables). At one point, she said something I didn't agree with and I looked at the guy across from me and rolled my eyes. It was a dumb move, and I immediately felt bad, so I did what I always do when I'm in a career pickle: I wrote about it on my blog. At the time I didn't think anyone cared about my site (NOTE: If you're in corporate, someone is always watching), and since I changed the names and a few other details, I thought I was safe. So you can imagine my surprise when a few days later I got a call from my coworker inquiring whether the post was about her. (Oops!) I'm a terrible liar—even little white ones—so I confessed, apologized, and yes, even groveled a bit. Still, our relationship changed after that. I mean, cold shoulder city. Did she have a right to be annoyed? Sure, but we still had to work together and her inability to let it go created a lot of unnecessary tension.

How to Recognize the Grudge Goblin. This one's easy. If the very sight or mention of a particular coworker turns on a finger-wagging, self-righteous diatribe about all the ways that person has done you wrong, you've got a grudge.

Take Action. For starters, stop taking everything so damn personal. There will be many times over the course of your career where you'll be irked by a colleague's behavior, attitude, or poor choice of words. It happens. Since he or she probably didn't mean to offend you, why make life more complicated than it needs to be? In fact, allow me to channel Oprah for long enough to tell you that when you hold a grudge, it holds you too. You can't pick your coworkers (if only, right?), so if you have a beef—deal with it head-on if you need to, then release it. You're not letting the other person off the hook, you're just not giving him or her any control over your attitude or behavior. See the difference?

CAREER-KILLER #3: WORRY

Not too long ago my mom had a suspicious lump on her breast that her doctor wanted to test further. Instantly, her mind took a Bolshoi Ballet leap to the worst-case scenario and she called me in hysterics, explaining—and I'm not kidding—how she wanted the money in her savings to be used for her funeral. Thankfully, the lump was benign, but the worry became a total mind-hijacker, and she was distracted and unfocused at her job for weeks. While a cancer scare is certainly serious, there are some people who apply that level of worry to *every little thing*, causing their brain to become endlessly distracted with "what-ifs" rather than *what's now*.

How to Recognize the Worry Goblin. Worry is defined as freaking out over things you can't control. At work, it could mean worrying about things like whether your proposal will win the bid, whether the presentation you just made was good enough, or whether your flight will be delayed. In short, if you find your mind is constantly asking questions that you couldn't possibly have the answer to, you've got a worry hob.

> **Take Action.** When your thoughts are racing with worry, all you have to do is stop and ask yourself one question: *What about this situation can I control?* Whatever that is, it's the *only* thing worth focusing on. Everything else has either already happened or might never happen. Regardless, worrying about it won't change the outcome.

■ ■ ■

Just being *aware* of any negative thought patterns (a.k.a. inner hobgoblins) can bring about tremendous professional growth because it's this awareness that reminds us *we* control our thoughts, not the other way around. So when you feel yourself headed straight for the negative, the grudge, or the worry in any given situation, remember that challenges exist to teach us something we didn't know before. And whatever it is, it's probably just the lesson you need to break through that inner glass ceiling and toughen up for the next level of your career.

woman 2 woman: *Knowing Your Worth*

"I've never had much time to focus on what I couldn't do. I'd rather focus on knowing my worth and being able to articulate it, which—for me—has always meant understanding how to build the fundamentals of a business. I know how to build operations and get the right players in place because, I don't care what you're selling, everyone follows the same rules. You have to understand the benefit of your product and then develop a team based on a common vision and what's best for the company. So, in that regard, I always delivered results. To me, that was my report card: What am I delivering—followed by what's my pay, what's my title, and how can I move within the company?

"I've always been fair and polite, but I've also made sure I knew—and the senior leaders knew—what I was bringing to the table from the very beginning of my career. I remember when I first started at MasterCard, I was in Chicago and the company headquarters was in New York. So when my boss would be asked to go to New York for an important meeting, I would make sure I came up with an impactful reason to be there, too. I knew what rang my boss's bell—and it was usually numbers—so I'd say, '*Let's consider the fact that this customer was at a 17 percent share and our team has them up to a 57 percent share. I'd be glad to go with you and give a presentation that demonstrates how we did it. Three quick points . . . boom, boom, boom.'* Then, after I met someone in New York, I'd keep in touch occasionally by sending info links I knew they'd find interesting, always copying my boss, so he didn't think I was jumping over him. Before long, I had influence and sponsorship within the company that stemmed from my initiative and ability to produce.

"Frankly, I was surprised at how fast my reputation flew through such a large organization. I'd go to meetings in Asia and people would say, *'Oh, you're Valarie Gelb.'* I built my confidence on what I achieved, and I didn't allow anything to hinder my potential."

—Valarie Gelb, former executive vice president/ chief sales development officer, MasterCard

if busy were the indicator of success, we'd all be billionaires

What are you doing right now *to change your circumstances so they are aligned with what you truly want for yourself?*
—Tory Johnson, workforce contributor for *Good Morning America* and founder of two multimillion-dollar companies, Women for Hire and Spark & Hustle

MEET TONIA.

As a corporate development director, wife, mother of two young girls, PTA leader, and board member for several non-profits, Tonia is a classic post-1970s feminist success story. She's at the top of her field, she takes her kids to school each morning, and she's at her desk by 8:30 a.m. every day.

In other words, Tonia is smart, driven, *and totally fried.*

If you were to bump into her on the street and ask *"How's it going?"* chances are she'll either dash past with a quick *"Crazy"* and a knowing eye roll, or pause for just long enough to tell you about her looming deadlines, overloaded inbox, and meetings she's running late for.

Tonia came to me a while ago because she felt overscheduled and underappreciated. She liked her job but felt stuck in middle management. She wanted to be a better mom but couldn't find enough time. She also wanted to be more "fulfilled". . . if only she knew what the hell that meant.

Tall order.

Tonia thought she would be more successful at work if she could tame her self-described "monkey brain," but the more she talked, the more it became clear that—deep down—she didn't want to. Calming the wild beast between her ears, even temporarily, would mean coming face-to-face with something she didn't really want to admit: Being a passenger in her career was a lot easier than taking the wheel.

Tonia didn't understand at the time that she was sabotaging herself by intentionally taking on too many projects at work, at home, and in her community—then turning around and using those projects as an excuse for why she hadn't achieved her own (vague) goals. She hid behind the idea that she was too busy, when the truth was *she simply preferred frenzy to fear.* Tonia was ambitious and had aspirations to move up at work, but as soon as she allowed herself to picture what success could actually look like (*"Maybe I do want to be VP"*), her mind would autopilot into "unknowns" that terrified her (*"Would I have enough time to spend with my girls? Could I make the budget and manage the team at the same time? Could I handle the stress?"*). Then, to justify her own fear-based decision to remain stagnant, she would convince herself that the opportunity wasn't a fit for her, anyway

("They'd probably want me to travel like Craig does, and I can't do that"). Secretly, Tonia knew that her uncanny knack for talking herself out of anything remotely uncomfortable is what kept her "stuck" in middle management. So, to satisfy her desire to feel respected without the risk, she threw herself into volunteering and leaned on "busy" like a crutch.

Sound familiar?

If so, you are on Tonia's track to burnout and gnawing discontent because—let's get honest here—*"busy" alone doesn't mean anything*. Monkey brain, scatter brain, mommy brain, and all the other useless blocks we allow to get between where we are and where we want to be don't mean anything, either.

> **To make significant *traction* (keyword) in your career, you've got to get rid of the mental clutter so you have space to unapologetically *define* and then *focus* on what matters most.**

Mental clutter includes the negative thought patterns from Chapter 1 (i.e., general negativity, grudge-holding, and worry), but it also includes overscheduling, overeating, overdoing it on social media, gossip mongering, wasting time, and all the other things we do to distract ourselves from what we *really* want. But here's the thing:

> **If you are living in chaos, it is being created by the choices you are making. Period.**

For example, Tonia *chose* her quasi-manic state by taking on too many nonprofit responsibilities. No one forced her to do that. Likewise, I've met other women (as I'm sure you have, too) who live in chaos because they *choose* to be everything to everyone else while bobbing at sea in their own lives. Hence they become the ever-multitaskers who may *seem* like they have it pulled together but secretly have eight Taco Bell wrappers on their floorboard and are still checking e-mail at midnight.

So let's stop with the faux success of "being busy" and focus on *how you want to feel*.

This was Tonia's cloud-parting moment because, once she recognized that what she ultimately wanted was to feel respected at work, she knew she had to stop searching for validation outside her job (*Aha!* moment No. 1). Therefore, her first step was to cut her community service to a more manageable level by focusing only on the two committees she felt most passionate about. This decision gave Tonia more "thinking time" (a.k.a. mental white space) to evaluate her career with a clear head. Eventually she realized if she stayed with her current organization there was a good chance she would always feel underappreciated, and no amount of community accolades would fill that void (*Aha!* No. 2). Tonia's story has a happy ending, though. She found a new job where she feels valued—as demonstrated by her shiny new title, salary bump, and boss who treats her like the goose with the golden egg. Still, it shouldn't have taken a break*down* for Tonia to have a break*through*.

Remember: Running isn't enough. The question you need to ask yourself is, *"Where am I going?"* The rest is just noise.

(To define what matters most to you, see Chapter 8, "Be More to Do More," where I detail a process for defining your virtues, intentions, and goals, or what I call a VIG list.)

CHAPTER THREE

reining in the mommy guilt

One's philosophy is not best expressed in words—it is expressed in the choices one makes . . . and the choices we make are ultimately our responsibility.

—Eleanor Roosevelt

LET'S GET ONE thing straight right away: If you choose to have a family, the notion that this is an "all or nothing" career decision is ludicrous at best, sinister at worst. That said, it does require sacrifices. There will be times when you have to leave work to deal with your kids and times when you have to leave kids to deal with your work. There is guilt in both, but you will save yourself a lot of heartache if you decide—up front—that "having it all" doesn't mean *being* it all. As discussed in the last chapter, if your every day is spent running full-steam from dawn until dusk, it's time to look in the mirror and admit that you're not serving yourself, your kids, *or* your career.

Let's change that. Starting now.

To begin, pick an evening, find a sitter, and meet with your partner for an honest assessment of non-negotiables. (NOTE: This advice applies whether you're married, a single parent meeting with an ex, or even if it's just you doing a self-assessment.) The time has come to decide which areas of your life, individually and collectively, will always be a priority and what is getting cut immediately—for now. Before your meeting, spend a few minutes completing this exercise:

Rate the following statements by circling a number from 1 (strongly agree) to 5 (strongly disagree):

My career has severely, negatively distracted me from my responsibilities as a mother.	1 2 3 4 5
My attitude and behaviors toward my child(ren) consistently demonstrate love and respect.	1 2 3 4 5
My attitude and behaviors consistently demonstrate my home life is a top priority.	1 2 3 4 5
My child knows how much I love him/her.	1 2 3 4 5
I tend to bark at my child(ren) more than I listen.	1 2 3 4 5
I make enough time to nurture and support my child(ren).	1 2 3 4 5
I frequently feel pulled in too many competing directions.	1 2 3 4 5

Based on your honest answers to each of these statements, you will know where to draw the boundaries in your life, albeit with an understanding that these boundaries will shift as your kids grow. For example, if you want to be physically present for your children while they're in school, it's not that difficult. Just grab the school calendar and—in one sitting—add the Christmas play, Valentine's party, pumpkin festival—whatever—into your calendar, then treat those events like unbreakable client meetings. You don't have to announce why you're leaving the office every time *("I'm off to Kaylie's school now!")* but you don't have to keep it a state secret, either.

As many parents have learned the hard way, if you wait for the school newsletter to update your schedule, you're just asking for trouble. *("OMG! There's a Mother's Day luncheon on Thursday? Like this Thursday?")* If you've ever made this mistake—errrr, guilty—you know what happens next. That's right. You're running around Target at the last minute on a frenzied quest for GladWare and cookies, secretly hoping you can put the cookies *in* the GladWare and pass them off as homemade. We've all been there, but if you're constantly having "OMG" moments of panic, it's time to get proactive about your schedule.

But more than just getting clear on what you plan to do, proactive scheduling also means getting clear on what you're *not* going to do. So if you're giving your all to your job and to your kids while they're in diapers, maybe that means you have to say no to excessive travel, joining the industry association, applying to grad school, or fund-raising for the library gala. So be it. These are the type of (hard) lines you have to draw with eyes wide open because you *will* be tested. Perhaps it's a close friend who promises that if you *juuuust* join the marketing committee she's chairing, all you'll have to do is attend a lunch board meeting once a month. She smiles, throws down the I-really-need-you card, and next thing you know you're stuffing envelopes in the middle of the night and writing donation checks with money you don't have.

Believe me, I understand the perils of taking on too much. When my boys were just two and four, I started a very demanding new job. As if that weren't enough, I also signed up for a leadership program that had me traveling out-of-town two nights per month for a year, I cochaired my city's young professional network, I served on a Habitat for Humanity committee, and I was writing my first book, *Effective Immediately*, "on the side." My breaking point was the night I received an e-mail from my new boss asking me to pack for a two-day strategic planning session with a few other managers. I could feel myself welling up and, then the *ugly* cry.

I'm not superwoman and neither are you.

At the time, though, I took on so much because I was terrified that if I put any of those amazing opportunities on the back burner I'd lose them forever. So I sucked it up. I ran fast, I ran hard and, yes, there were a number of evenings where I'd come home only to stare at my sleeping boys, having missed a whole day of their young lives. For me, those moments stung the most because I felt completely victimized by the demands on my time. I wasn't clear about what was negotiable and what wasn't, so everyone else's need felt like my call.

It took me a long time to realize the need is NOT the call.

If you have kids, *they* are—although it doesn't have to be at the expense of your career or anything else you feel passionate about. So . . . as you are building the fence around your schedule, think about the following.

Sanity 101: Five Must-Have Tradeoffs for Working Moms

TRADEOFF #1: GO FOR THE "BIG MONEY"

In other words, what can you do that will be the *most* important, the *most* visible, and have the *most* impact? When it comes to prioritizing time, your kids aren't all that different from your boss in this respect. If they are old enough, just ask them. For example, you can say, *"It looks like I can make only one school event this month—either the lunch or the assembly. Which one would you prefer I attend?"* The fact that they have a voice in the decision will help your kids feel better about it—not to mention they're learning a valuable lesson in time management, too. Also, if you're on a crazy airtight schedule, don't allow yourself to get talked into *anything* behind-the-scenes. You may get a gold star from the PTA for selling the most raffle tickets, but your son or daughter probably couldn't care less. So before you commit to something, think about whether your child will notice. If the answer is no, well, there's your answer.

TRADEOFF #2: KNOW WHAT'S IMPORTANT TO YOUR KIDS, EVEN IF THEY DON'T TELL YOU

If your child senses you are completely stressed out, he may downplay the significance of things he really does care about. It could be the school field trip you blew off, but it could also be something of greater significance, like unwanted peer pressure or the rejection of a first crush. The way your kids need you has as much to do with what's going on in their lives as what's happening on the "family calendar," so you can't get out of tune with them—regardless of how full your inbox is.

TRADEOFF #3: SCREW GUILT

It's nothing more than shooting yourself in the face for falling short of what you think you should be doing. Did you catch that? Guilt is *self-induced*. So put down the gun. The only thing that matters is the relationship you have with your child, and if that's all good, everything else is all good. The comparison game isn't worth it because there will always be moms who seem to juggle life effortlessly and still make time for Zumba. If your version of "success" is based on who made pecan sandies from scratch or who spent the most time volunteering, you'll never win because you'll never feel good "enough."

Here's a tip: If you still can't shake your guilt, try keeping a journal of your finer parenting moments. You'll not only have something to bring you back around when you feel completely hopeless, but you can give it to your kids as a memento down the road. (Ha! History is written by the victors, remember?) Also, you're probably not going through anything a little malbec and a lot of trench stories with other working moms can't fix. So schedule a girls' night ASAP. Trust me, it's way cheaper than therapy.

TRADEOFF #4: PUT THE ENDGAME FIRST

Just like you do at the office, focus on details without losing sight of the bigger picture. Are your kids happy and well adjusted? Again, if your relationship is strong and they're not in juvie, who the bloody hell cares if no one had a hot breakfast this morning? "Mom Capital" has deposits and withdrawals all the time, but if no one's in the ER and the house didn't burn down, life is good. Parenting isn't a day-by-day or week-by-week gig, so forgive yourself (and your boss) if you occasionally have to miss out on something cool because your job needs you. (Take it from someone who missed the kindergarten graduation ceremony of her first born.) If your kids are old enough, use the occasion to explain that you are responsible for something at work and you want to do your best so that you can be proud of the result—and yourself.

TRADEOFF #5: UNAPOLOGETICALLY GUARD YOUR CALENDAR

It's often a bellwether of your happiness. (Really.) So think about that the next time someone asks you:

To join a committee you're not passionate about

To go to lunch when you really don't want to

If it's okay to "*pick your brain*" over coffee

As a very successful friend of mine often says, "If the answer isn't *hell yeah*, it's NO!"

> **woman 2 woman:** *On Parenting ~~vs.~~ and Career*
> "To be honest, my children didn't see a lot of me in the first few years, and I personally think the earlier years of my kids' lives were easier for me to work. As long as they were taken care of, I was fine. Now that they're older, I feel like they need me to be there more. Most working moms start out home with their kids and go back to work. My schedule has been the opposite."
>
> —Liz Lange, maternity wear
> pioneer and designer at Target

"Ambition and motherhood often felt like rivals in my first years as a new mother trying to have it all. I had a career by choice and I wanted to grow, advance, and be the leader I felt I could be. Yet, I also wanted to join my first-grader for parents' lunch, have family dinners together—most of the time—and be there for soccer. I was constantly turning the dials to do both on my terms. And while my story is still being written, it's coming along nicely.

"I'd love to say I had a master strategy to get me to this point, but it's been more instinct and some small decisions along the way that really mattered. I have never worn my Mom card 'on my sleeve,' but I felt it was my issue to manage in my private choices and decisions.

"I made it a priority to work for leaders I knew would respect my choices, and I constantly negotiated roles and situations to fit my life. When I was approached about a new role, I was clear that I had some realities and priorities that they should understand up front. And I had my own internal 'line in the sand.' I made a few decisions to pass on some great opportunities because it crossed my line— but not many. I also treated my sons' events with the same respect as if they were critical client meetings. When a meeting was being scheduled on a date that conflicted with the fourth-grade class party, I just said I had a conflict that day and we usually found another option. Over time, I learned that I had more control than I thought I did.

"Let's be clear. I didn't do this alone. I had a wonderful nanny when the boys were younger. We live in a neighborhood that lives by the philosophy, 'It takes a village,' and my husband and I still have a Sunday night ritual of comparing calendars to confirm who can cover car pool, doctor appointments, or pick-up at a friend's house. Ambition and motherhood on my terms have ultimately been compatible—at least on most days. I feel that I have been there for our two boys, but they have also seen their mom follow her dreams, too."

—Patti Johnson, chief executive officer, PeopleResults, and former chief people officer, Accenture

"Do not lean back [in your career], lean in. Put your foot on that gas pedal and keep it there until the day you have to make a decision [regarding family], and then make a decision. That's the only way, when that day comes, you'll even have a decision to make."

—Sheryl Sandberg, chief operating officer, Facebook

"The toughest career challenge for me has been balancing work and life, which I'm sure many women can relate to. I have a daughter who is grown now, but for much of her childhood I was juggling raising her and growing my career. Over the years, I learned that you can have it all—just not at the same time. I passed on some career-advancing opportunities while she was in high school so that she could complete all four years in one place—and I don't regret a minute of it. You have to make one thing a priority and achieve balance that way, rather than trying to do everything all at once. We all have a finite amount of energy and time to give and must figure out the best way to have an impact on the things that matter to us most—and it's okay that each one of us will do it differently."

—Jan Fields, president, McDonald's USA

"I'm the CEO of a global organization with almost 20,000 employees, and I've got four children at home. So, for me, there's just work and family—nothing in the middle—and there is no balance. It's all a juggling act and I'm constantly making sure that all the balls are in the air and that I don't drop any. I have an unpredictable schedule and I'm usually on conference calls beginning at 6:00 a.m.—because that is the time I can talk to our teams in Europe, India, or Australia—and I'll work until 8:00 or 9:00 at night. I don't manage from an ivory tower, and I work really hard to understand all the issues, local, regional, and global. However, to be this hands-on means that I'm traveling to our facilities around the world one-third of the time. While I consider Friday night to Monday as family time, I do understand that our family dynamics are not typical. My husband and I have had to teach our children that they have been given opportunities and exposure to things most children do not get, but it comes at a price. I tell them that because my position affords them those privileges, I have to work really hard. It's a double-edge sword."

—Heather Bresch, CEO, Mylan

CHAPTER FOUR

om the job

how to beat stress and anxiety

Peace. It does not mean to be in a place where there is no noise, trouble, or hard work. It means to be in the midst of those things and still be calm in your heart.

—Anonymous

STRESS IS DEFINED as an anxious state where the pressures we face exceed our ability to cope. Obviously, this is a huge issue that both men and women face; however, the American Psychological Association says women regularly report *higher* levels of stress than men.

Why?

Turns out, there's much debate on this topic. Some people say we're too "busy." (Remember that?) Others say we're simply more attuned to our own well-being—or lack thereof. Still others say we have a propensity to keep our feelings buttoned up, resulting in even more anxiety overall. *(Thar she blows!)*

How do you deal when you're feeling completely stressed? Do you suffer in silence? Lash out? Retreat into a tub of cookie dough? While these options are certainly common, none of them are ideal, and none will serve you well in your career.

If your goal is to effectively lead others, you must manage yourself first—which means understanding how to get your personal stress/chaos meter within a normal range.

Just like the engine gauge on your car dashboard, your personal stress meter will read high sometimes and low sometimes— but the trick is being able to bring yourself back to a healthy, neutral point so that you can continue to function efficiently.

This is where Eastern philosophies truly excel. At their core, practices like yoga and meditation are remarkable stress busters because they teach the art of self-examination through self-discipline. It's like the old saying, *"The harder you are on yourself, the easier life is, and the easier you are on yourself, the harder life is."*

This idea is critical when it comes to stress, because often what we feel is the self-generated result of taking it too easy on the front end, causing more anxiety on the back end. For example, we wait until the last minute on deadlines, leading to overtime, short fuses, the inevitable printer breakdown, and the downward spiral continues. We stress about our bodies but eat the pastry anyway . . . which leads to feeling guilty, which causes more stress. See the patterns forming?

The good news is that since the majority of our stress is self-induced, it can be self-eliminated. We've already discussed the importance of releasing the (literal) headlock of inner critics and "busyness" on our lives (see Chapter 1); another tool you can use in this process is the art of mindfulness. If you're thinking, *"Hold up there, granola girl,"* don't worry. I'm not asking you to run out and join an ashram.

Being mindful simply means paying complete attention in the present moment, a skill that is dying on the vine faster than typewriter repair. Mindfulness is about focusing—perhaps for the first time—on how you truly live, with an enhanced understanding of everything that's right in front of you *right now*. While this practice can make all aspects of your life more enjoyable, the impact of mindfulness on your career is especially profound. For example:

- You'll lose the urge to react instantaneously to your own thoughts and feelings, resulting in better decision making.

- You'll be able to handle stressful situations in a calm, collected manner, resulting in increased executive presence.

- You'll be more appreciative of what you have (instead of constantly focusing on what's missing), resulting in a heightened sense of personal well-being.

As many professionals have learned the hard way, the things we tend to bungle at work usually don't stem from a lack of *intelligence*, but rather a lack of awareness when it comes to the feelings behind our actions and the actions of others. That's why mindfulness should be at the very center of your career strategy. Because when you are fully present, you become highly attuned to the *perceptions* driving behaviors, which, in turn, drive results. For example, maybe you're not really stressed because your boss is a jerk, but because you frittered away an hour on Facebook and now you're behind on the CRM report. Or maybe your colleague isn't really impatient with your ideas because she thinks they're all duds, but because the meeting you called is running 15 minutes over and she has a conference call to prepare for.

I promise that once you understand that the root of *everything* is perception, you will work in a completely different way. Here's how to cultivate your own mindfulness, starting with the simplest steps and working your way up to mastery.

Keeping in Mind @ Work

STEP 1: BE MINDFUL OF YOUR BREATH

Most people take short, shallow breaths that only get shorter and shallower under stress. Therefore a simple and decidedly painless way to begin "awareness" at work is through mindful breathing. It starts like this: Take four or five loooong, deep breaths every couple of hours. Feels good, right? That's because deep breaths naturally clear out stress by increasing oxygen flow to vital organs . . . no mask (or tank) required.

STEP 2: BE MINDFUL OF YOUR SURROUNDINGS

In *Effective Immediately*, Skip Lineberg and I wrote that "cluttered desk = cluttered mind." Still true. How can you possibly focus with toppling piles of paper everywhere that only make you anxious every time you catch a glimpse of what you have yet to do or file? Not to mention, what kind of message are you sending to others about your ability to handle your current projects?

Treat outer junk as a symptom of inner junk.

In other words, get rid of clutter on your desk so you can focus on creating a space that allows you to focus on your work without triggering a paper avalanche.

STEP 3: BE MINDFUL OF HOW YOU'RE TREATING YOUR BODY
The Centers for Disease Control reports that more than one-third of U.S. adults are obese! Holy cow. *How did we get to this point?*

Since we spend the majority of our days in the office, a big culprit is obviously mindless eating at work. Think about it: So much of what we shove in our mouths on the job is driven by convenience—snacking on leftover bagels from the IT meeting, grabbing a handful of candy as we swing by the reception desk, using soda as a mid-afternoon pick-me-up. (True story: I used to work with a woman who drank *four* regular Cokes a day. Four! That's *10 teaspoons* of sugar, people!)

I'm not writing a diet book here, but I definitely think it's worth noting that none of this stuff is your friend. I know it's difficult and unpopular at times to be the person with the discipline to say "no" when everyone else is saying, *"Oh, c'mon! It won't kill you."* (Obvy, these people are trying to make themselves feel better about eating the sleeve of Thin Mints.) A treat here and there probably won't cause a coronary event, but the point is that when you are *consistently* mindful of treating yourself better, you will feel better, you will look better (hello, confidence!), and as a result, you *will* work better. Period. Not to mention that when you're strong physically, that strength tends to bleed out into all areas of your life.

STEP 4: BE MINDFUL OF WHAT YOU'RE WORKING ON IN THE MOMENT

We pride ourselves on being able to multitask, but the truth is, our brains don't have the capacity to focus on two things at once. It simply can't be done. So spend your time on *single tasking* instead. Make it a rule to give all you have to the project that's right in front of you—and forget everything else until it's complete or you have to move on.

Note: When you're feeling totally overwhelmed, this process becomes even more critical. You may want to freak, scream, kick your cat, or shut down entirely—but to what end? None of those options will help your to-do list shrink any faster. So when you find yourself in full-on panic mode, just keep breathing deeply and saying to yourself, *"One hour at a time. One day at a time. One project at a time."*

Day-blocking is a good strategy for overall calendar control (as discussed in Chapter 11), but if you are in immediate crisis mode, pull out a timer and commit to one solid hour of work on your highest-priority task. This means no e-mail, no social media, no quick check-ins with your phone, no thoughts of *"I'm totally drowning here"*—nothing. For this one hour, it's just you slaying the dragon. At the end of the hour, spend 15 minutes or so catching up on your inbox and responding to text messages, then *set the timer again* for another hour and go right back at it.

Through this process you are retraining your mind to focus on the work instead of the worry about the work.

You *will* get there, one hour at a time, one day at a time, and one project at a time. That's all you can do and, as long as you're giving your best, that's good enough. Put your focus on what matters most and what you can control. Then, let the rest go.

STEP 5: BE MINDFUL OF YOUR STRESS TRIGGERS

When you're aware of your personal stress bombs, you can plan *for* them instead of react *to* them. Typically, this step will require a shift in perception. For example, at the beginning of my career, I worked in an office where we had Monday morning staff meetings and everyone was expected to report on the status of their projects. If one of my tasks was overdue, I often found myself getting anxious and testy with my manager. At the time, I didn't have the self-awareness to understand my "frustration" was actually mischanneled guilt for missing my deadlines.

Over the years I've learned that to be mindful of how we react under stress, we have to be mindful of what is causing it in the first place. Nine times out of ten, our reactions have less to do with the situation itself and more to do with the story we tell ourselves about it.

When I reflect back on those Monday morning meetings, my "story" was that I was being attacked, which made my inner hobgoblins (see Chapter 1) come out swinging (*"Geez, I'm doing the best I can here!"*) and so my behaviors followed suit. My fuse was shorter, my body language was combative (crossed arms, death stare—you get the idea), but it was all just my perception of the situation back then and not what was really going on. In reality, my boss was just asking simple questions about timing while I sat there steaming like a jackass. If I had just changed the story in my head from *"Why is he coming down on me all the time?"* to *"He's just doing his job and trying to see where I need help,"* I could have avoided a public demonstration of behaviors that made me seem erratic and unprofessional. Get it?

If you want to change your results, change the story you're telling yourself.

Positive perception = positive behaviors. Negative perception = negative behaviors. Which do you think is going to get you promoted first?

To be effective in your job, you have to be centered and collected. All business gets crazy at times, and so you must know how to process the million things that are thrown at you each day in a way that is not only calm *but inspires calmness in others.* How will you know when being mindful is working? Simple. Your anxiety will disappear, your relationships will be drama-free, and you won't recall the last time you had a mascara-smeared crying jag in the company bathroom. Believe me, if you're staying cool when a coworker tries to one-up you (again) in front of your boss, when you have a to-do list that's completely out of control, or when you have to deliver the board presentation without sweat rings down to your knees . . . it's working.

As you would expect, there are nuances to mindfulness that go much deeper than I have space to cover here, but if you find yourself making a genuine connection with the practice of being present, I strongly encourage you to *go even deeper.* Get a coach, attend a retreat, or take an online course. The more you reach out and connect with like-minded (pun!) individuals, the richer this experience will be. All you need is a *tiny* amount of willingness to change and you will be amazed at how the teachers appear and the doors of knowledge open.

Action Plan: Self-Awareness Goals

Select three goals from the following table and write them in the career plan template provided as Tool 1 in the Section 6 Toobox. (For an e-version of the career plan, please visit www.emilybennington.com/templates.)

Action	Points
Wake up one hour earlier each morning for one month and use the time for inspired reading and personal reflection. Spend 10 to 15 minutes of this time in focused breathing and setting your intentions for the day ahead.	15
Parents, either meet with your partner or define for yourself the areas of your schedule(s) that are "non-negotiable." Decide where you are *choosing* to spend time and what can be cut immediately, knowing your boundaries will shift as your kids grow.	15
Join or start a mastermind group where you and two or three other women leaders share advice and hold each other accountable for set objectives.	15
Limit TV to one to two hours per day for 30 days, ensuring that whatever you do watch is actually worth your time (i.e., free from all the behaviors you're trying to avoid).	15

Spend a week monitoring your thoughts, actively trying to "catch and release" negative patterns. Remember: The only way you can silence your inner critic is to understand it's not real. *Any* thought that doesn't propel you forward is meaningless and should be given no weight or value whatsoever.	10
Take a five-minute "brain break" in your office every day for one week (i.e., turn off your phone(s), close your e-mail, close your eyes, focus on your breathing, and relax).	10
Take a class in yoga or meditation.	5
As a symbol of your commitment to change any roadblock habits along your personal career path, take a moment to post this message on your computer: TODAY MATTERS. FOCUS ON THE ESSENTIALS. (Go to www.emily bennington.com/art to download a JPEG version.)	5
Create a career vision board full of inspirational quotes and photos. (Add 10 bonus points if you're brave enough to hang it in your office.)	5

1	2	3	4	5
Self-Awareness	Social Skills	Personal Effectiveness	Team Development	Leadership
	↑ You are here.			

Core Principle

You enjoy harmonious relationships at work because you are a force of positive energy who can be counted on to "show up" professionally, communicate with respect, and (when needed) disagree without being abrasive.

In this section, you will learn how to:

- Navigate three top sand traps for executive women.

- Put the kibosh on competition.

- Handle inappropriate advances appropriately.

What Your Coworkers Are Thinking

"Wait, I really like *Amanda."*

CHAPTER FIVE

indirect, emotions, and tears (oh, my!)

Don't wait until you get the powerful career to inhabit the space of a powerful person.
—Marianne Williamson

AFTER COUNTLESS wine-fueled conversations with girl-friends on whether they preferred working for a man or a woman—and, frankly, not liking what I was hearing—I decided the topic was going to be a cornerstone of the research for this book. So when I surveyed 700+ (presumably sober) executive women and asked them the same question—*"Would you rather work for a man or a woman?"*—the responses were also disturbing.

First, the good news: More than half of the respondents (56 percent) said gender didn't matter. Here's a snapshot of their comments:

"I want a smart boss."

"My preference depends on character rather than sex."

"I just want a good leader."

Now for the bad news. Are you sitting?

Of the remaining 44 percent who would actually choose their boss based on gender, 32 percent would select a man and only 11 percent would select a woman! That's a *three to one* margin, folks, although many of the respondents at least had the decency to be conflicted, remarking, for example:

"I have always preferred to work for a man . . . but as a feminist I feel guilty about that."

Maybe you've heard of previous studies with similar findings and felt conflicted yourself. On one hand, labeling women managers as inferior only perpetuates the same hackneyed stereotypes (again) that continue to hold us back. On the other hand, everyone knows the only way to really bring about change is to fearlessly smoke out whatever is "wrong" so that it can be fully addressed.

Since it's the things we ignore, avoid, and intentionally keep hidden that eventually hurt us the most, if there is a certain negative bias against women leaders, isn't it better to shine a light on it instead of pretending it doesn't exist?

Problem is, the loudest and most influential dogs in this fight are often the most derogative. As a result, women have been pinned as too weak, too aggressive, too manly, too sexy, too girlish—even too queenly. Ever heard of the Queen Bee Syndrome? Some women actually claim to experience psychological pain and suffering under the direction of other women managers. (Google it.)

Of course, all of this begs the question: *"Are professional women really this bad, or have we been so duped by the media that we're actually looking for the worst in ourselves?"* Either way, something's up. So let's get our hands dirty and sort through the yuck.

Here are the top three reasons the women surveyed for this book would rather work for male managers.

Why Surveyed Women Preferred Male Bosses

REASON #1: MEN ARE MORE DIRECT

"I usually find male bosses easy, effective, no nonsense."

"I hate to say this but . . . my male bosses have been easier to read and made expectations clearer than most of my female bosses."

—Survey respondents

Overwhelmingly, the women surveyed who preferred to be managed by men justified their selection by stating men were simply more direct. In fact, there were a few distinctly indirect personality types that participants identified as exceptionally frustrating, including:

The Chicken. The Chicken is someone who avoids uncomfortable conversations at all costs. Often, she hides behind e-mail. As an example, I had a manager tell me the story recently of a chicken who was summoned to his office for a bit of corrective coaching. Since she was usually a spirited staffer, he was surprised when she sat in mousy silence as he explained how she could have handled a particular situation better. At the end of the meeting, he asked the employee if she had any questions. She didn't . . . *and yet* . . . not even an hour later he received a long and laboriously detailed e-mail from the employee stating her side of the case. It was, in his words, "*absolute madness,*" and definitely lowered the employee's stock at the firm. (For more on how to effectively communicate in person, see Chapter 14, "Solve the Freakin Problem!")

The Chicken Little. This is the coworker who takes *everything* as an affront. Out of coffee in the break room? Chicken Little immediately goes on the defensive, insisting it wasn't her job to order it. Ask John's opinion in the sales meeting? The Chicken Little assumes it's because you don't value hers. *Whatever* the situation, she'll find a way to turn it around and make it personal. If this sounds familiar (constantly offended = big red flag), there's a good chance your colleagues really are annoyed with you. So the next time you feel yourself getting your feathers ruffled, stop and think, "*Am I making something that's not about me . . . about me?*" This question will help you see the whole pie rather than getting myopic about your little slice because—the truth is—very little of what goes on in your office is about you. Also, if you take offense easily, it could be because you're insecure about something in particular—so you need to get curious about what that is. For example, if your inner critic has you convinced that you're a dimwit, you may get irked when someone else's feedback is solicited, and even though it may feel like anger, it could actually be *insecurity*. Likewise, if you're annoyed because your boss is spending more time with another colleague than you, the Chicken Little mind will scream "favoritism" as opposed to acknowledging what's really going on, namely, *jealousy*. Again, it's only when you get honest with yourself about what you're truly feeling that you can take the right steps to fix it.

The Wimpy Delegator. Women have a high degree of empathy, which tends to translate into weakness when it comes to delegation. (*"Oh, you're working on the Smith brochure? That's okay, I'll come back later."*) While it's fine to be sensitive to the workload of others, it can't always be at the cost of getting your own stuff done. (Plus, I'm sure you've never met anyone who pretended to be oh-so-busy to avoid working at all, right?) Assuming you are delegating a task with sufficient turnaround time, you have every right to hand it off—without apology—and let your coworkers figure out the best way to prioritize their time. The first part of that sentence is key, though: If you're always the person with the hot potato assignments, coworkers will understandably get frustrated eventually. Also, even if you do have the luxury of lead time on an assignment you're delegating, be sure to set an official deadline with your coworker—ideally one that gives you an extra day or two of padding. Yes, I know the deadline dance can be the most awkward part of delegation, but if you avoid it, then what happens? You might assume your colleague will go back to his desk and start working on your project right away, while he might assume that—since you didn't mention the deadline—it's not a priority. See where this is going? (If you have a problem with coworkers who constantly miss deadlines, see Section 4 on team development and the subsection "How to Handle Tricky Team Situations @ Work.")

The Bunnytrailer. The Bunnytrailer is the person who starts off on one topic but then—*ooohhhh, shiny object*—gets easily distracted: *"This reminds me of that conference in Paducah a few years ago . . ."* By the time the Bunnytrailer wraps up her "point"— *"Do you know what I mean?"*—you're totally lost. And plum worn out. So . . .

If you want to get noticed at work the fastest, be the person who communicates the clearest.

Simple as that. Of course this means no using 500 sentences when five will do, no using sesquipedalian words (like I just did), no forcing coworkers to keep up with bouncing-all-over-the-place ideas, and no waiting for an "uh-huh" or head nod as your signal to stop talking.

This is where your *mindfulness* will help (as covered in Chapter 4), because it teaches you to be v-e-r-y comfortable in quiet. When you find yourself drifting off on a tangent, it helps to think, "WAIT," which is not only a direct reminder to take it down a notch and get yourself centered, but is also an acronym for *Why Am I Talking?*

Oftentimes when we speak, it isn't because we have something insightful or overly profound to say but because we are so uncomfortable with silence we're usually thinking and yapping at the same time.

Obviously, you don't want silence to waft in the air like a bad smell, but the time has come to seriously rethink normal pauses in conversation. We call them "awkward" and make them taboo, when it should be perfectly fine to take a few extra beats if it means a more thoughtful response is being formed. If you're having difficulty with concision, try watching TV pundits. They only have about a minute (or less) to answer each question, but note how they present key ideas and—importantly—how they wrap each point declaratively (even when they're dead wrong). You can also take a crash course in Japanese business etiquette where it's not uncommon at all for executives to stew over an idea for a full 30 seconds (or longer) before responding. Were that the norm across the globe, it would be a small price to pay for the gaffe-fest we call office life.

REASON #2: MEN ARE LESS COMPETITIVE

"Unfortunately, women come to the workplace feeling so scrappy, as if they have to fight for everything as they try to climb the ladder."

"My experience with women has been almost all competitive."

—Survey respondents

A few months ago I was having breakfast with a friend of mine who had just returned from a national meeting where all of his company's regional leaders were asked to make short, five-minute presentations to their peers and C-level officers, including the CEO, CFO, and COO. This was an $8 billion, global organization, so it's always a big deal to have that kind of face time with the executive team. Still, I almost spit out my coffee when my friend told me how one of the regional leaders introduced his idea to the group and then said, "*I think the best person to talk about this is the guy who drives it for our group. Dave, c'mon up here.*"

Problem was, Dave had *no idea* he was going to be called up to give the presentation, so . . . slightly beet red in color . . . he stuttered and stammered his way through, completely off the cuff. Now, Dave—despite his lack of extemporaneous speaking skills—had a fabulous reputation in the company and was well known for being a rising star. Therefore, the question on everyone's mind was: Did the manager put Dave on the spot just to make him look bad?

As my friend told this story, I was struck by how casually he recounted the facts, like it was no big deal. Meanwhile, I'm thinking, *"What an asshole! If I were Dave, I would be so mad!"* This was a reminder that men have a tendency to see competition as a semi-routine part of business whereas women seem to have the antenna way up for any slight or perceived injustice.

And while my intention is not to debate whether women are more competitive than men, I can say that on the survey for this book, it showed up. A lot.

So here's the deal: If you're playing a bitchy comparison game, then you're completely screwing yourself because you'll always be somewhere between "not good enough," which is debilitating, or "better than," which is egotistical. Either way, you're constantly seeking validation based on things you *do or don't have*. In Section Three, we're going to develop a much better system for evaluating your success than tit-for-tat thinking, but just to be clear, I'm not saying that you shouldn't be *ambitious*, only that you don't need to measure your achievements against everyone else's.

Your success doesn't limit others any more than their success limits you. To think otherwise is to choose to be little—and littleness won't make you happy *or* successful.

For more on this topic, see Chapter 6, "Competition (Yeah, Let's Talk About It)," and Chapter 8, "Be More to Do More: Creating Your Virtues, Intentions, and Goals (VIG) List."

REASON #3: WOMEN ARE TOO EMOTIONAL

"Women tend to bring emotions to the table no matter what, and can be unfair because of that."

"Women bosses can be dramatic and remember the smallest perceived slight forever."

—Survey respondents

Why is it that, in situations where we (both men and women) need to demonstrate the most emotional maturity, we seem *least* equipped to handle it properly? For example, let's say you are trying to explain to your supervisor that you're feeling over-whelmed and—sure enough—here come the tears. You're mortified (*"Aaaak! I'm crying in front of my boss!"*) but feel powerless to stop it. Turns out you have more control than you think, but—once again—you have to understand your behavior before you can control it. And since it all starts in your mind, let's take a quick tour.

First Stop: The Prefrontal Cortex (PFC). Otherwise known as the "executive function" of your brain, the prefrontal cortex is responsible for your overall problem-solving and decision-making abilities. You know how your brain lights up on MRI scans like dopamine fireworks when presented with photos of spa treatments, raspberry chocolate ice cream, and Lake Como? (Or maybe that's just me.) When your brain is under stress (say, when you're having a tough convo with your boss), the prefrontal cortex actually reduces its activity. In other words, *it's not functioning properly—so neither are you!* Of course, this should be backflipinducing good news, because when you understand there are biological reasons why you act the way you do, you won't think you're crazy. *You're not crazy*—your mind is just hypersensitive to what it perceives as overly stressful situations.

Second Stop: The Amygdala. For those of you who feel like your mind is routinely in high-anxiety mode, it's important to know the culprit is most likely your internal fire alarm, otherwise known as the amygdala part of your brain. You need the amygdala because if you are in serious danger (say, you're being mugged in an alley), it's what tells you to panic *immediately*. Unfortunately, if you're uncomfortable at work, your amygdala—doing its thing again—will also tell you to panic *immediately*. It's not all that great at distinguishing between mortal fear and routine stress, which is why most people aren't either. But here's the rub: If you are constantly responding to your body's stress signals, you will constantly be shooting at a quail with a cannon. In other words, you will *always* be overreacting. So the next time you're in a situation at work where you feel your heart start to pound and the adrenaline kicking in, understand that it's just your amygdala doing its job. Assuming you're not in any real danger, you don't have to react like you are.

Attention Crybabies!

For both genders, the prefrontal cortex and the amygdala tend to function similarly; however, there is something else going on when women are stressed that you need to know about.

A few months ago I interviewed former Nickelodeon Vice-President Anne Kreamer about her fabulous book *It's Always Personal: Emotion in the New Workplace*. In her book, Kreamer notes that all humans have a hormone called prolactin, which, among other functions, is thought to be our "crying trigger." (Basically, when the prolactin is flowing, so are the tears.) But get this:

> **Women have *six times* as much prolactin in our bodies as men. In addition, our tear ducts are *twice* as large as men's, which explains why we tend to gush tears and men tend to trickle.**

So think about the effects—literally—of our bodies at work. Between the executive function (prefrontal cortex) that dims, the amygdala that panics, and the prolactin that waterfalls—honestly, is it any wonder we are perceived as more emotional? As a former walking emoticon in the office, I used to think that my outbursts of tears or fury—while occasional—meant that I was less stable, more irrational, and not as capable of leadership roles as the men in my office. When I realized I wasn't weaker—just hardwired differently—it was a true parting clouds, God beam, angels singing, head-smacking, "*Hallelujah!*" moment.

Of course, I'm not suggesting women have a license to carry around a box of Kleenex, because intense emotions on either end of the spectrum clearly make coworkers highly uncomfortable. However, this little biological crash course is still something to celebrate because it is further proof that *you are not your thoughts*—you are the *driver of your thoughts*. Subtle difference. Massive impact.

CHAPTER SIX

competition (yeah, let's talk about it)

It is what it is, but it will become what you make it.
—Anonymous

MISTY COPELAND had overcome a lot since she began taking ballet—in a gym, not a studio—at the relatively late age of 13. While she showed prodigy-level talent, the fact that Misty was a teenager meant she had to work especially hard to compete against ballerinas who were practically en pointe as toddlers. (It's easier to mold that famous "dancer's body" before it's fully developed.) Still, determined to give it a shot as a professional, Misty spent an "intense four years" eating, sleeping, and breathing dance. She was en pointe within 12 weeks (something she now calls *"really dangerous"*) and training six days a week, up to six hours a day, not including evening rehearsals, performances, and—you know—*school*.

At 17, Misty was thrilled to learn her work had paid off. Out of 150 students in the summer-intensive program of the prestigious American Ballet Theatre in New York City, only 12 had been invited to be part of the company—and she was one of them. It was a dream opportunity, especially since ABT was home to her longtime idol, Paloma Herrera. Since Paloma had traveled the dancer's career ladder from corps-to-soloist-to-principal in just under five years, Misty assumed this would be her path, too. But three years came and went with no promotion. Then another year passed, and *another*. Misty was routinely working 10- to 12-hour days, but she was still in the corps . . . and she was starting to get nervous.

Why Do Comparisons Trip Us Up So Much?

Maybe you're not quite off the psycho-meter just yet, but if you constantly find yourself ranking your success against the achievements of other people, you've still entered dangerous head space, mama. Since it's hyper-easy to get swept up in the comparison game without even realizing it, let's just call this out right now for what it really is: Another dirty mind spiral.

Playing the victim, allowing jealousy to run rampant, and stewing helplessly over your own unmet desires won't do anything more than erode your confidence. It won't solve any problems or put you on the path to achieving your goals any faster. It will, however, unleash a particularly insidious wave of insecurity—one that's super-crafty at keeping you stuck and playing small.

It's also important to realize the comparison game is an ego assignment. When you're ambitious by nature, it's easy to assume that someone else's pie has to get smaller for yours to get bigger. It's also easy to assume that if someone else has reached a goal faster than you, that person must be better. Not true. What *is* true, however, is that if you allow your mind to wander down these unhealthy paths, your behavior will start to reflect your thoughts in very unhealthy ways. You may start to act competitively at work—perhaps withholding information that would be valuable to a colleague—or you may even be so discouraged by someone else's success that you feel compelled to give up entirely. (*"They've already beat me to the finish line, so why should I even bother?"*)

At this point, you have two choices: get angry or get inspired. You can allow your jealousy to percolate within, raging to the surface when you blame poor circumstances, no resources, or just plain old bad luck for why you haven't achieved the life you want. (You'll know you've hit this wall, by the way, when you feel a growing darkness in your heart, and every success your "competitor" has—even tiny ones—are like a nail being pounded right into it.) Alternatively, you can choose to convert your envy into inspiration.

You can choose to celebrate remarkable, fabulous colleagues—in both your office and your industry— for showing you what is possible for yourself.

So, if you feel your mind drifting back to a place where you're wondering whether so-and-so is prettier or smarter—or lamenting the fact that she is younger, more connected, more accomplished, with more followers, etc.—it's time to get out your big ol' mental hammer and whack those thoughts into submission. Remember: Even though the world is constantly telling you otherwise, success is a pie with an infinite number of slices. As long you take great care to find role models who have risen to the top with their moral compass intact, you have no reason *not* to be happy for them—*just as you'll want others to be happy for you.*

Begrudging other people's success only takes up brain power that could be better used to cultivate your own. Not to mention, if you're really honest with yourself, you're likely to find your anger isn't about them, anyway. *It's about you.* It's pent-up, misdirected resentment against yourself for all the things you're not doing that they are. The good news is the solution here is relatively simple: Get moving. Forget petty comparisons and turn the focus inward on what you are doing to bridge the gap between where you are now and where you want to be.

This is exactly what Misty Copeland did at the American Ballet Theatre. Recognizing that stewing over her career wasn't accelerating it, Misty, in her own words, "got serious again." She dug deep, shut out all of the external baggage, and recommitted to her training with the same intensity she had shown as a teenager trying to break into the business. Her boss took notice and later said in an interview that he saw "an edge" in her work that had been missing for some time. After seven years in the corps, Misty was finally promoted to soloist.

Jealousy offers clues to something you ultimately want for yourself.

So, don't run from it or, worse, soak it in bitterness. Instead, pay attention to your envy. Sit with it. Ponder what it is about someone else's career that triggers this feeling inside you. Then reverse-engineer their success. What, specifically, have they done to get where they are today? What personal habits have contributed to their accomplishments? Social media is great in this respect because it becomes like a glass wall, giving you instant access to how your role models spend their time. My guess? It ain't sulking. The more *action* you take for yourself, the less tension, anxiety, and frustration you'll feel toward those who've already achieved what you're reaching for. Your goal is merely to get to a place where you can be genuinely happy for their success. After all, they're lighting the way for you, too.

The Real C-Word

Competition. We all do it. We measure ourselves against what others have or have not achieved (and by when) in their lives. While this can be motivating for some of us, for others the competition becomes all-consuming and, as a result, completely unprofitable. Remember: Whatever you project onto others, you only strengthen in yourself.

Fortunately, there are a couple of relatively easy tricks you can use to pull the shoot before a tiny comparison becomes a full-blown mind virus.

COMPETITION CRUSHER #1: STOP IT COLD

Whenever you find yourself mentally conjuring up something you don't want in your head, simply think *"judging"* or *"next!"* That's it. The goal here is to completely shut down any comparisons before they have a chance to take root. This process may not come easy or naturally at first, but stick with it and repeat as needed.

COMPETITION CRUSHER #2: IMPOSE A FILTER QUESTION

One of the hallmarks of being truly mindful is the ability to ana-lyze yourself thought-by-thought. This is the real work of life change because it requires you to stop—in the moment—and think, *"Is this thought (or action) getting me closer to who I want to be?"* If the answer is "yes," carry on. If it's "no," see #1 above.

seriously, don't bring sexy back

LAST FALL I HAD the privilege of speaking at a women's leadership conference where Gloria Steinem was the keynote. When asked about whether the feminist movement was over, she softly replied: *"I don't know why women aren't more angry these days . . . because we still have so much to be angry about."*

As I scanned the crowd of more than 3,000 executives— women who were college educated, sitting on boards, and running multimillion-dollar companies—it was easy to wonder how a room full of successful alpha-femmes could possibly be angry. (Okay, *aside* from being judged as indirect, competitive, and emotional.)

But, of course, there is something else . . . something as powerful and volatile as a fault line running just beneath the surface of "relations" at work. Yep, I'm talking about sexual tension, and if you've felt it in the workplace, you're not alone. In fact, of the women surveyed for this book, 68 percent said they have been hit on in the office. While there were a few tales of true love sprinkled in the mix of comments (*"I married him and glad I did!"*), most of the time when the sexual fault line erupted, it was decidedly unwelcome:

> *"A coworker crossed the line in both visual looks and not respecting personal space. He left shortly after I raised the flag to a supervisor. It took a lot of courage on my part, but I did not feel that it was taken seriously. Perhaps it was management's inability to know how to appropriately handle the situation."*
>
> *"He grabbed me and I slapped him. I quit."*
>
> *"I was an expert witness in the courts and a judge put his hand on my knee and made a suggestive comment. We were supposed to be on a professional lunch."*
>
> *"I was young and new to the job and he took advantage of my vulnerability. Not that I am blameless, but . . ."*
>
> —Survey respondents

This is a delicate tight rope for us girls, huh?

Let's take looks, for example. On one hand, we can argue all day long about whether it's fair or politically correct, but it still won't change the fact that we live in a society where appearance matters. (In one of the many studies on beauty and work, economist Daniel Hamermesh concluded that *"plain people earn less than people of average looks, who earn less than the good-looking."*)

Now, on the other hand, if you've been lucky enough to hit the genetic lottery—or if you're just really good at faking it—you've probably noticed that sending libidos out of control can actually *hurt* your career. It's one of those things that, at first, seems pretty sweet. Maybe you get invited to more events and meetings, or maybe you become a confidante to a senior-level exec. However, assuming you don't fall into the category of those who go on to have healthy, long-term relationships, this movie has a predictable ending:

1. You alienate other colleagues who take offense to your methods of getting ahead. Or,

2. You go "too far" and ruin your reputation altogether.

So here's where the *responsibility of beauty* kicks in. That is, it's okay to be beautiful (you can't help it, after all); what's not okay is using your femininity in a sexual way to garner attention at work.

There's a thin line between being beautiful and being sexual. One is what you *are*; the other is how you *act*.

That said, there will be times when you are not instigating anything and *someone else* is trying to turn your office into singles' night. What do you do then? While every situation is different (translation: there are no cookie-cutter solutions; you must do what is right *for you*), there are a few general guidelines I'm going to recommend (noting that your comfort level is always the benchmark of what's appropriate and what isn't).

If your boss, client, or colleague makes a sexually suggestive comment (usually disguised as a joke), but you *don't* feel uncomfortable . . . let it go.

You don't have to laugh—in fact, it's better for all of us if you didn't—but it's entirely possible the dirty jokester has no idea how offensive he's being. (Sad, but true.) If you *occasionally* (keyword alert) bump into this behavior from peer-level colleagues, the best thing for you to do is tolerate it (although I'll add a caveat to that in just a few moments). I know it isn't fair and many of you will read "tolerate" as synonymous with "condone," but the unfortunate truth is that there are career repercussions for throwing down the bias or harassment card, so you don't want to kick that particular hornet's nest until you have to.

In the meantime, one of the *worst* things you can do in the midst of sexual "humor" is to jump in. For starters, your attempt at a joke could be misinterpreted by someone else. But more than that, if you do need to approach HR down the road, you don't want your own potty mouth to be used against you. (And here's that caveat: If you are the manager, you cannot tolerate or ignore this behavior. As the leader, you have an *obligation* to call out even the most casual sexism.)

If your boss, client, or colleague makes a sexually suggestive comment and you *do* feel uncomfortable . . . you've got to speak up.

First, give the person a bit of rope to wiggle out of the situation by saying something like, "This conversation has gone down the wrong road," coupled with a firm I'm-not-kidding look. If that fails, you should come right out and say you are uncomfortable and you'd like to keep it G-rated. If *that* doesn't work, you may have no choice but to go to your supervisor if you're dealing with a client or colleague and ask to be reassigned.

However, if the culprit *is* your boss and you've given ample warning (oy vey!)—*now* you need to head to HR. As I mentioned previously, though, going to HR—particularly about your boss—is sure to open a big can of worms, so be prepared. For example, your boss will most likely say that you're overreacting (if not outright lying), and it's a safe bet the company will take his side since he outranks you. Therefore, you'll need some proof in the form of written communication or a witness—although the latter will be tough, since most of your colleagues won't want to burn down their own barn. In addition, you'll also need to be able to account for any behaviors of your own that could be considered even remotely suggestive. For example, did the boss come on to you while you were both drinking at a bar after hours? That doesn't make his behavior right, but it certainly doesn't help your case, either. What were you wearing at the time? There are a few items we view as perfectly normal office attire—dangly earrings and tight, button-down shirts, for example—that men find overtly sexy. Again, I'm not saying it's right, just calling out the facts because—while there's a chance you may have a perfectly fair hearing with no long-term career damage—there's also a chance that raising a stink could effectively derail your locomotive at work, and yes, that is something we should *all* be angry about.

woman 2 woman: On Harassment

"I was hit on by the head of another department who was working with my boss. In truth, I think my efforts to dissuade him were half-assed since I will confess, in retrospect, it was flattering. That said, I felt trapped, like I had no easy options, and that no matter what I did, I'd piss off someone who could potentially affect my career. I finally did have the wherewithal to extricate myself. Today, I'd have more presence of mind and the confidence to set clear boundaries. Rookie mistake."

—Dani Ticktin Koplik, founder of dtkResources

"Getting hit on in a professional setting is a reality for many women, so we should all be open and honest about the fact that—yes—it does happen. The choice you are faced with is how you choose to handle it—or not. The reality of the situation is that men and women are human. Almost everything we do in life and business is because there is some level of interest and chemistry in it, otherwise we wouldn't do it, right? And that's attractive!

Businesspeople are full of vision, commitment, and life. It's part of doing business. However, by no means am I suggesting that if you find yourself in an uncomfortable situation that you shouldn't move to resolve it. I am simply saying that to focus on someone in business being attractive is just human. Regardless of what anyone says, getting hit on is simply a fact of life. It just is.

"That said, I wouldn't be honest if I didn't tell you that especially when I was starting out and trying to prove myself, I found it pretty disheartening to be in meetings where it was clear that the person I was meeting with cared more about what I looked like than what I actually had to say. My worst experiences were in speaking with investors only to be met with sly smiles and 'light' questions, followed by a dinner invitation or, even better, a flat-out date request. I knew what was going on, but I was too young and inexperienced to realize that, rather than letting it get to me, there are other ways to handle it.

"These days, as a married woman, whenever I find myself getting hit on I quickly put things in perspective. I don't make a big deal of it, but I do stay *very* focused on the agenda I have for the meeting. Also, I am hugely supportive of women, but I am also about being fair and taking personal responsibility. The guys do get a bad rap, but I have often seen women—myself included at times over the years—in a situation where the person sitting across them at the table is someone they're interested in dating. In other words, we need to be honest with ourselves that 'being hit on' can go both ways. But if you don't want to blur the line, for example, don't wear the low-cut shirts and high skirts. You are asking for it, and we both know that's the case. Instead—if you want to be taken seriously—dress the part. If you are doing business, then do business. There are lots of beautiful skirt and pant suits that help keep the focus on what you have to say rather than how you look. You will forever be faced with lots of noise in the workforce—including being hit on—but stay in charge. This is your life, your plan, and your career."

—Ingrid Vanderveldt, M. Arch, MBA, Dell Inc.

How to Handle: Tricky Social Situations @ Work

When: Coworkers want to dump their work on you.

You Should: *Be wary.* Oftentimes, people will attempt to get out of their own projects by appealing to your ego. They'll claim you are "really talented," so you're the "best person" to handle the job. If whatever they are asking you to do is legitimately within your job description, then smile and get started.

However, if you know these coworkers are just trying to flatter you into doing their work, ask them to put their request in writing. You could say, for example, *"No problem. I'm in the weeds on the Mercer project right now, but I'm happy to help you out. Can you send me an e-mail with the scope and your deadline? I just need to finish up a few things here and I'll get back to you by the end of the day."* At this point you have four choices:

1. You can do the work and hope your coworker doesn't pull this trick again—which, of course, she will.

2. You can request a meeting or phone call to explain that you'll help this time, but you have your own assignments to complete and working on her projects may cause you to miss your deadlines.

3. You can politely refuse—maybe offering to help on a small piece of her project or to read through the final report as a consolation prize, but not do the work. (Don't be stupid. This is *not* an option when dealing with someone who outranks you.)

4. You can forward her written request to your supervisor for input and advice on how to handle. Warning: Be *careful* before you break this seal. If the supervisor goes directly to your colleague, she will feel betrayed and will most likely want to punch you in the neck. Therefore, your first step should always be to try to resolve any issues directly with your coworker, bringing in your supervisor only as a last resort.

When: You've been given a totally unrealistic deadline.

You Should: *Employ "polite pushback."* If the assignment is coming from your boss, chances are you'll have to bend over backward and get it done. That said, if this is a reoccurring problem, you should gently broach the subject (in person if possible) as it happens by saying something like, *"I'll get started right away. Is that a hard deadline, though, or do you have any wiggle room because these reports usually require extra research and I want to make sure I have time to get it all covered."* Tone is everything here because you don't want to seem like you're reprimanding your boss—even though you kinda are.

If the assignment is coming from a colleague and you know you can't meet the deadline—*don't agree to it.* No one likes conflict, but you'll either have to deal with it now or later when you're late on the task, so better to tackle it up front while you still have a bit of leverage. (Once you sign off on a deadline, it's on you to meet it.) Assuming the coworker doesn't usually have such tight turnarounds, the previous script should work (see "When coworkers want to dump their work on you"). However, if this is yet another rush job, you should take a pause and add, *"Lisa, is there any reason why we are always reacting to these things last minute?"*

Again, tone is everything (which is why you need to have these conversations in person or, worst case, over the phone). You want Lisa to feel as if you're "in the trenches" too, because, truth be told, there's a good chance she's only enforcing a deadline given to her by someone else. If Lisa feels you are being judgmental or disrespectful, she will most likely go on the defensive, so you have to make the request as if you're trying to get to a workable solution for both of you. This situation requires some professional diplomacy—and it's a tough conversation, for sure—but it's one that needs to be had in the beginning and not the middle of the project or, rest assured, you both will limp to the finish line.

When: You've been assigned a project you don't agree with.

You Should: *Try a divide-and-conquer strategy.* In other words, see if you can persuade your colleague to break up the project into smaller pieces where you can essentially test its validity. Initially, you probably don't want to let on that you hate the concept, so try saying something like, *"Since we're starting from scratch here, I'm not entirely sure how long this will take. How would you feel about reassessing after the mailing list is complete? We'll have a better sense of scope then."*

It's worth noting here that—especially in corporate life—there will most likely be a lot of projects or assignments you don't agree with. Some of them may not make sense to you directly but are vital to other parts of your organization. So if you're going to be a voice of dissent, be sure to pick your battles wisely and—as any military general would say—make sure it's a hill you're prepared to die on. In other words, since you obviously don't want to build a reputation on push back, when you do speak up, it better be something you feel very strongly about.

When: Colleagues take credit or claim your work as their own.

You Should: *Get strategic.* First, if you know you have a *really* good idea, don't run it by your entire department before presenting it to the boss. The more watered-down it becomes, the less likely it will be remembered as yours.

Second, if your boss wants to take your idea to the team or, better yet, *his* boss, push to be included—whether it's being present at the meeting or in on the e-mails. In this case, your boss will most likely be the one taking the lead here, with you doing all the background work and research. There's no sense in getting frustrated, but there is something extra you can do. Give your boss everything he needs to excel (after all, you *want* the idea to be adopted) but save a few arrows for yourself. In other words, have some supporting facts and anecdotal stories in the hopper that you can pull out when the time is right.

Also, it's important to accept the fact that you won't always get credit for every contribution you make. That's business. Your boss is probably more concerned with how he looks to his boss than with making sure you are properly acknowledged. As long as it isn't the norm *all* the time . . . just be patient and roll with it. You're making yourself indispensable *now*, which is leverage you will be able to use later. Plus—and this is a biggie—by not demanding to be recognized *every* time for *every* little thing, you are sending a message that you understand the bigger picture, which is critical to your ability to move up.

When: Coworkers love to gossip.

You Should: *Engage* only *if it affects the business.* If the gossip is related to your core business (e.g., Are competitors trying to poach your clients? Are employees looking for new jobs? Why is Fred constantly taking a two-hour lunch?) it may be helpful to listen to it. After all, you want to be aware of anything coming down the pipe that could affect your market position or strategy. The line you don't want to cross, though, is making decisions based on gossip or hearsay. So, if you find your team is creating Plan A around "what if" scenarios that are much better suited for Plan B, take a cue from politicians and make it clear that you want to deal only with facts, not speculation. (Seriously, watch our elected representatives ramrod "what if" questions—it's masterful.) While you always want to have some basic contingency planning in place should any overly threatening rumor prove true, don't fall into the trap of reacting to nothing. Whenever there is a decision to be made, ask *"What are the facts here?"* and build your plans around what's real—and *only* what's real.

If the gossip is petty, personal in nature, or otherwise unrelated to your core business, then bust out the blatant change of topic. That is, simply ignore the gossipy comment while quickly changing the subject. For example, if your colleague says, *"I can't believe Kim gets to go to London for the training,"* you say something like, *"Yeah, what a great opportunity for her. By the way, do you know the new deadline for the Ford budget?"* Remember:

People only want to gossip with you if you make it fun for them by reveling in all the salacious details. When you don't engage, it's not fun—and they'll get the hint eventually.

When: You're on the receiving end of a very inappropriate advance.

You Should: *Reread "Seriously, Don't Bring Sexy Back."* (Chapter 7).

When: Your coworkers are unresponsive.

You Should: *Ask for forgiveness instead of permission.* If you've given colleagues repeated attempts to weigh in and all you've heard back are crickets, you have no other choice but to keep your projects moving forward. So make the best, safest choices you can—without completely overstepping your authority—and then be prepared to defend them with real, substantive facts when called upon. Hopefully, you won't find yourself in this position too often; however, if it's *always* like pulling teeth to get others to contribute, you're probably in the wrong work environment.

When: Coworkers are always throwing cold water on your ideas.

You Should: *Try good old-fashioned diplomatic persistence.* So you were expecting a standing ovation, but all you got were tomatoes. It happens. Still, if you truly believe in your idea, there are a few ways to get heard, namely:

1. *Be prepared.* It's easy to argue with opinions, but hard to argue with facts.

2. *Build a coalition.* A team of supporters is tougher to defeat than a Lone Ranger. So be sure to seed your idea to key stakeholders in advance of your pitch meeting or e-mail (while also heeding the advice above on "When colleagues take credit or claim your work as their own"). The right coalition will not only help you cultivate a support network, it will also serve as a mini focus group where you are free to kick the tires prior to your official pitch.

3. *Continue to speak up.* If coworkers are poo-pooing your brilliance, maybe it's not the idea that's flawed, but the way you're presenting it. Take a moment to switch gears, pinpoint a new benefit, and take another swing. You did think through the potential hurdles, didn't you? If so, this should be easy.

4. *Assess whether it's your idea or just the work style of the other person.* For example, if colleagues are asking a lot of probing questions about your proposal, you may begin to think they don't trust you when in reality they just like to process lots of information. Once again, it's easy to make something personal that isn't personal. This is where you have to stop and become acutely aware of the stories you are telling yourself because your behavioral reaction to the thought, *"This is just how Rick works,"* is going to be quite different from your reaction to the thought, *"Rick doesn't like my idea and is trying to make me look bad."* Get it? Don't be a victim when you don't have to be. Check

your story first and deal with the facts, not your perception of the facts.

5. *Get some better ideas.* Who knows? Maybe they're right. We all have a tendency to fall in love with our own ideas, and sometimes it takes an outside perspective for us to snap out of it and see that perhaps *every* pitch won't be a home run—and that's okay.

When: Your supervisor is a micromanager.

You Should: *Empathize.* That's right. Try to see where he's coming from. Maybe he had a micromanager boss and has simply adopted the style. Or maybe he's been burned by employees in the past and has trust issues. Regardless of the cause, it always helps if you make an effort to *understand* your colleagues first before you demonize them.

Next, it's critical to understand that micromanagers are looking for one thing—comfort—so give it to them in the form of overcommunication. This is where Friday Updates really rock the party. All you have to do is send your boss a quick, bulleted e-mail each week outlining your:

1. Accomplishments

2. Areas where you need further input

3. Goals for the week ahead

Keep your Friday Updates very short and simple, because there's a good chance your supervisor is micromanaging *everyone else* and, well, that just sounds exhausting.

Action Plan: Social Skills Goals

Select three goals from the following table and write them in the career plan template provided as Tool 1 in the Section 6 Toolbox. (For an e-version of the career plan, please visit www.emily bennington.com/templates.)

Action	Points
List your top three personal "stress triggers" (e.g., clutter, running late, procrastination, overscheduling, out-of-control inbox, lack of exercise, etc.) and develop a plan for how you will avoid or react to each of them. This doesn't have to be a 15-tab spreadsheet. Just jotting a sentence or two in a journal—or other prominent place where you'll see it frequently—is enough.	15
Informally ask your boss and a few trusted coworkers for feedback on your communication skills—specifically, your ability to get to the point, delegate effectively, and respond without getting emotional. Needless to say, you are opening the door for some constructive criticism here, so remember what a gift this really is. When you know better you do better, but you can't do better if you don't know. (You might need to noodle on that for a minute.)	15
Surely, if Martin Luther King Jr., Gandhi, Nelson Mandela, and the Dalai Lama can control their anger, there's hope for the rest of us. Read a biography on one (or all) of these nonviolent icons and learn how they channeled anger without becoming bitter.	15
Get to know different people in your office by inviting a new colleague to lunch every week for one month (10 bonus points if you invite your boss).	15

Step up to a companywide call for help on a volunteer project (10 bonus points if you get your project covered in an internal blog or newsletter).	15

Create your own affirmations to call upon when you are about to pop like a corn kernel from stress, anxiety, or frustration. For example, spend a few minutes repeating one of the following sentences in your mind: *"I can only control myself," "I am willing to let go," "There is another way to see this,"* or *"One hour at a time. One day at a time. One project at a time."* If these thoughts don't work for you, create a statement of your own that helps calm you down when needed. — 10

Read *Crucial Conversations: Tools for Talking When the Stakes Are High* by Kerry Patterson. — 10

Read *It's Always Personal: Emotion in the New Workplace* by Anne Kreamer. — 10

Record the birthdays of important work colleagues and clients in your calendar and send them each a card or small gift. (Note: It helps to buy a few cards/gifts at once so you're not always rushing around at the last minute. And, no, Facebook posts don't count as sincere birthday greetings.) — 10

Next time you attend a professional event or reception, introduce yourself to at least four new people (10 bonus points for following up with a "nice to meet you" e-mail). — 10

Don't let an inappropriate advance catch you off-guard. Think about how you'll handle it when (yes, *when*) it happens. — 5

Purchase a large piece of foamcore and put it in your workspace with markers. Ask colleagues to write their favorite quote on it.   5

Strategically place a few other conversation starters in your office. For example, chuck the family portrait (yawn) in favor of a picture of everyone zip-lining in Costa Rica. Have a quick story handy for all of your office decor (e.g., photos, books, action figures, etc.) and, once your neighbors are tired of your stories, rotate in new decor —and new stories.   5

Bring in bagels and/or (good) coffee for your floor— just because.   5

While at a companywide meeting, make an effort to sit with folks you don't know.   5

Stay late for a colleague who is swamped but has an after-work obligation.   5

Make it a point to know the names of your colleague's children—and ask about them often.   5

part two
call in the good stuff

When you clear out what doesn't serve you, you create space for what does.

Section 3:
PERSONAL EFFECTIVENESS

1	2	3	4	5
Self-Awareness	Social Skills	Personal Effectiveness	Team Development	Leadership
		↑ You are here.		

Core Principle

You have a clear understanding of your personal virtues and a way to measure progress on how well you achieve them. In your job, you not only deliver what's asked of you on time and on budget, but you regularly bring new ideas to the table as well. You have a solid grasp of your individual success metrics and consistently engage in training and development to stay razor-sharp in all aspects of your performance.

In this section, you will learn how to:

- Identify your core virtues.

- Cultivate value-driven habits.

- Own your career.

- Earn respect on the job.

What Your Coworkers Are Thinking

"Wow, Amanda knows her stuff."

CHAPTER EIGHT

be more to do more

creating your virtues, intentions, and goals (vig) list

I didn't really know what I wanted to do, but I knew the woman I wanted to become.
—Diane Von Furstenberg

I HATE the phrase *"work/life balance."* It's rubbish. "Life" doesn't stop when you're in the office and, if you are like most people, "work" doesn't stop when you're at home. For too long we've been trying to measure the success of one part of our lives *against* the other, which usually causes us to fail at both. So let's focus on something else.

Let's focus on becoming our highest and best selves, regardless of whether we're in the office or at home.

The VIG Life

Goals [Future Self]

Intentions [Present Self]

Virtues [Evergreen Self]

That's where the VIG list comes in. Short for Virtues, Intentions, and Goals, the VIG list is essentially a life roadmap, providing clarity and direction for *all* the areas that matter most. That said, this roadmap probably looks a little different from others you've been exposed to. That's because the element that drives most plans—namely, goals—has less influence here. Indeed, to the outside world, success is found amid a pile of achievements and checked boxes. That's where most people and books will tell you to spend your time.

I say that's a recipe for *unhappiness* if ever there was one.

It's dangerous to use goals alone as a blueprint for how your life is supposed to pan out. They rarely unfold according to our plans (or our schedule!) and, as a result, we get frustrated and discouraged. That's not to say having goals isn't healthy. Goals are absolutely critical to keep us moving forward—which is why they appear at the end of every section in this book. But the thing about goals is that they constantly keep us focused on a *future* outcome. When your ability to feel "successful" is wrapped in goals, you can't get anywhere fast enough, so you spend the majority of your time trying to prove yourself, be somewhere else, and get to that ever-elusive next level.

This is why goals alone are pretty unfulfilling. Sure, it's an awesome high when you achieve them, but then what happens? The bar moves up and you set more goals. Of course, if you *don't* meet your goals, well, then you feel like a loser. Again and again, we end up measuring our success by what we did or didn't get, by what we do and don't have. This is the wrong focus.

> **Don't anchor your happiness around goals, anchor it on virtues instead.**

Rather than focusing on the things you want to achieve someday, focus on the qualities you want to embody right now, in *this* moment, and every moment beyond.

Virtues: Your Evergreen Self

"Evergreen" means something classic that isn't married to any particular trend or season. For example, when a photographer says she wants a shoot to be evergreen, she means don't come rockin' a thick winter sweater or feather hair extensions. In the VIG life, virtues are the foundation on which everything else is built—they are the "evergreen" you, unchanging even as your goals and accomplishments come and go. I like to use as my template Benjamin Franklin's list of 13 virtues, which he developed at the ripe old age of 20 and pursued for the rest of his life.

Talk about timeless.

Franklin's virtues are just as relevant today as they were when they were written in 1726. *And that's the point.* If Franklin had simply created a list of goals (Lighting rod—check! Independence—check!) we would not still be talking about his list centuries later. The people, technology, and whims of the world will always change and evolve, but core values will remain the same. Why would you ever want to focus on anything else?

Benjamin Franklin's 13 Virtues

Virtue (The What)	Intention (The How)
1. Temperance	Eat not to dullness; drink not to elevation.
2. Silence	Speak not but what may benefit others or yourself; avoid trifling conversation.
3. Order	Let all your things have their places; let each part of your business have its time.
4. Resolution	Resolve to perform what you ought; perform without fail what you resolve.
5. Frugality	Make no expense but to do good to others or yourself; i.e., waste nothing.
6. Industry	Lose no time; be always employed in something useful; cut off all unnecessary actions.
7. Sincerity	Use no hurtful deceit; think innocently and justly, and, if you speak, speak accordingly.

8. Justice	Wrong none by doing injuries, or omitting the benefits that are your duty.
9. Moderation	Avoid extremes; forbear resenting injuries so much as you think they deserve.
10. Cleanliness	Tolerate no uncleanliness in body, clothes, or habitation.
11. Tranquility	Be not disturbed at trifles, or at accidents common or unavoidable.
12. Chastity	Rarely use venery but for health or offspring, never to dullness, weakness, or the injury of your own or another's peace or reputation.
13. Humility	Imitate Jesus and Socrates.

By his own admission, Franklin fell short of this list on many occasions; however, he didn't allow his imperfections to throw him off entirely—nor did he allow a focus on virtues to thwart his ambition. (Obviously.) Instead, he used his virtues like a personal GPS system to keep him on a righteous path.

Taking Franklin's cue, I created my own virtues to live by, and at the end of this chapter you'll find a template to do the same.

My 11 Virtues

Virtue (The What)	Intention (The How)
1. Spiritual Growth/ Strength	Be a seeker in life, constantly searching, learning, and listening.
2. Family	Put my family first; parent proactively; model patience, love, and respect.
3. Discipline	Eat and drink in moderation; commit to daily exercise and meditation; maintain and complete a daily to-do list; react thoughtfully.
4. Positivity	Read something inspirational each morning; catch and release attack thoughts; practice forgiveness; disengage in littleness or gossip.
5. Mindfulness	Be present in the moment; savor happiness; hug more; embrace and share joy; savor meals without rushing; accept responsibility for my part in all relationships.
6. Cleanliness	Maintain order in personal appearance and environment, including workspace, home, purse, and car.
7. Serenity	Maintain a peaceful mind through life's small problems and big sorrows; never shout in anger; attend a retreat annually.
8. Industry	Minimize time wasters; follow

	through on all promises; meet dead-lines; avoid procrastination.
9. Patience/ Detachment	Release expectations on how things should turn out and when.
10. Love	Practice kindness; release judgment; offer encouragement; give freely; volunteer to help; nurture relationships; seek understanding of all; see divinity in all.
11. Courage	Be honest, even when it's tough; model integrity; stand up for what is just; don't listen to critics; get uncomfortable; follow the path fearlessly.

Intentions: Your Present Self

Intentions are the action steps you take *in the present moment* to live your core virtues. If you are confused about the difference between intentions and goals, here's the deal: Goals are concerned with future outcomes, while intentions keep you grounded in the here and now. As such, you should spend the most time and energy—by far—on intentions.

The question to keep in mind here is, *"If I didn't know you, how would I know?"*

In other words, how would someone who just met you know that the virtues you've identified are the areas that really float your boat? For example, if you listed "serenity" as one of your virtues but are constantly snipping at your colleagues (or your kids), you're not living your intentions, are you?

Likewise, if you listed "courage" but you're a church mouse in the office, that's not jiving, either.

It's not a virtue if you don't live it.

To be honest, we typically give ourselves way more credit than we deserve when it comes to judging our intentions vs. our actions. My friend and leadership consultant Buddy Hobart likens this to the difference between watching a Hollywood movie and seeing a film clip. As we evaluate our own behavior over time, it's natural to look back on the "whole movie" and feel confident that our good qualities and performance have far outweighed any bumps along the way. That said, when others are asked to evaluate us, they will most likely think in terms of "clips," which are snippets of our behavior, and usually the most dramatic ones at that.

This disconnect explains why people who are technically good at what they do, but not very savvy in terms of interpersonal skills, are often completely dumbfounded when they don't get the promotions or leadership positions they feel they "deserve."

Typically, they're judging themselves on the whole movie (e.g., *"I've been here five years."*), while others are judging them on clips (e.g., *"Janelle always takes the last cup of coffee and never makes another pot. That's so rude."*).

If you understand how to align your virtues, intentions, and actions, you have the key to unlocking major changes in your behavior. Whereas 99.9 percent of the workforce will make decisions based on how they think and feel at any given moment, *you'll* be making decisions based on what you really want for yourself. There's your power, girls.

Goals: Your Future Self

Yes, we need goals. This very book lists goals at the end of most sections because without them, we would all be a bunch of drifting, aloof, quasi-productive navel-gazers. The cliff to avoid, however, is when you become so attached to your goals that your entire sense of success and happiness is rooted in whether or not you achieve them. This is why I recommend living by the following:

> **Spend 70 percent of your time pursuing virtues and intentions and 30 percent pursuing goals.**

For those of you who may be thinking this advice is "too soft" for the realities of the workforce (a.k.a. an ambition-killer), let me remind you that 30 percent is not an insignificant amount of time. *It's one-third of your life.* So, no, you don't get out of working your ass off and, yes, big dreams, big intensity, and big commitment are still the price of admission for a big career. I'm certainly not saying virtue isn't without wealth. I *want* you to be über-rich and über-powerful, but I also want you to have the foundation to handle that kind of success when it arrives.

So . . . Now It's Your Turn

Create your own Virtues, Intentions, and Goals (VIG) list using either of the two templates provided below. (For e-versions of these templates, visit www.emilybennington.com/templates.)

Virtues and Intentions List (70 percent of your time)

Virtues (The What)	Intentions (The How)

Virtues (The What)	Intentions (The How)

Once your virtues and intentions are outlined, now let's add in the goals:

- Pick your top three goals from the end of the first five sections in this book. These are the goals most relevant to your career path *and* that you pledge to complete within the next 60 days.

- Write them in the Career Plan Goals template below.

- At the end of the 60 days, add all your points and assess your "promotability" using the separate template provided in Section 6: Toolbox.

▪ Once you've completed all of your goals from this list, guess what you should do next? That's right—set more!

Career Plan Goals List (30 percent of your time)

Exercises	Points	Completed Date
Self-Awareness		
1.		
2.		
3.		
Social Skills		
1.		
2.		
3.		
Personal Effectiveness		
1.		
2.		
3.		
Team Development		
1.		
2.		
3.		

Exercises	Points	Completed Date
Leadership		
1.		
2.		
3.		

At the end of this process, you'll be able to put the pieces together for a very solid life and career plan. In fact, you'll not only have a to-do list, you'll have a to-*be* list as well. (How cool is that?)

Still, putting your VIG list on paper isn't enough. To see real change, you have to *live* your virtues, intentions, and goals each day *and* measure your progress. In the next chapter you'll learn how to do just that.

CHAPTER NINE

building VIG-ilicious habits

If we were as industrious to become good as to make ourselves great, we should become really great by being good.

—Ben Franklin

SUCCESS—AS DEFINED by accomplishment that is both achieved and sustained—obviously doesn't just happen to lucky people. It happens to those who know where to draw the line between "wanting" and "doing."

"Wanting" is like "trying"—both are crutch words designed to make us feel as if we're making progress when in reality we're still stuck. The more you *want* something, the more you *try* for it, the more elusive it becomes.

Case in point: If everyone who *wanted* or *tried* to lose weight actually did, there would be no obesity epidemic in this country. The parallel career epidemic, however, is that there are millions of women who *want* and *try* to move up at work, only to find the same success on the corporate ladder that they do on the bathroom scale. (Which is to say, none.)

The good news is that you already have everything you need to succeed—you just need a new way to tap into it. This is where your habits come in—or what we're going to affectionately refer to as your career "practice."

Ever heard of the word *sadhana*? If you're a yogi I'll bet you have. Sadhana is a Sanskrit word that translates to dedicated, daily action employed to reach a specific goal. Note the word *daily* because regardless of whether your practice is on the mat or in the boardroom, a true sadhana is a constant process of growth with no clear beginning and no clear end. Same thing in your career.

If you want to put your car in forward and hit the gas at work, you will have to put forth the time and energy required *every single day* to see results. This process is exactly like mindfulness or going to the gym—you're never quite "finished," only temporarily done for now, and it takes a deep reservoir of discipline to stick with it and see results.

Right now you may be thinking, *"I'm not all that great at self-discipline and—if I were—I wouldn't still be trying to lose that weight, smartass."* Believe me, I get it. This is where the mental conditioning we learned about in "Section One: Self-Awareness" comes in handy. To get your mind pointed in the right direction, start thinking of yourself on a daily path to professional growth.

In fact, the single most transformative thing you can do for yourself professionally—ever—is to genuinely view your career as a *practice* and consistently set aside 15 to 20 minutes every day to reflect on where you've been and where you're going.

Problem is, most people don't take their career growth seriously enough to work on it outside work. For example, a *Yahoo!* survey of nearly 3,000 web visitors found that 60 percent had not read a career or professional development book in the past year. Huh? (Kudos to you, though, for reading one now!) This is symptomatic of a deeper problem facing our society today: We tend to run away from anything remotely uncomfortable, even if it's ultimately good for us. But . . .

The path of least resistance is the path of mediocrity and regret.

So . . . assuming you're onboard with the mindset of a career sadhana—that is, you are ready to go to work on yourself—you're probably wondering *"What now?"* To get started, grab your Virtues, Intentions, and Goals list from Chapter 8. Then develop your own accountability system using one of the scorecards I've provided below. Don't overwhelm yourself by attempting to tackle everything at once. Just pick a format that's manageable to you. I recommend you start off with the weekly sheet (Scorecard A) for a few months to immerse yourself in the process, then zoom in to the more detailed sheet (Scorecard B), as needed, for the virtues or goals you want to work on. (For electronic versions of these forms, visit www.emilybennington.com/templates.)

VIG-ilicious Scorecard A

You can create a template similar to what Ben Franklin did by listing your VIGs vertically down the left column and the days of the week across the top. Then, check in with yourself daily by placing a ✓ (*Woot!*) or an **X** (*Shucks!*) where they meet. Same rule applies, though—brutal truth! If you find that you are constantly bumping into the same walls, you have to be honest about it so you can get to the root of the behavior or change a VIG that's not right for you. Either way, you've learned something, so you win.

	Sun	M	T	W	Th	F	Sat
Virtue 1							
Virtue 2							
Virtue 3							
Virtue 4							
Virtue 5							
Goal 1							
Goal 2							
Goal 3							

VIG-ilicious Scorecard B

To go in for the kamikaze-dive of accountability, list your VIGs down the left column and rate yourself on how well you are achieving them at the micro level using a 1 to 5 scale, where 1 = outstanding and 5 = work on it, sista. Again, the way to get results here is not only to do the work, but to be super-honest about it. So, if you gave yourself a 1 or a 5 in particular, write down the *specific* behaviors that are working for or against you in the notes section of the scorecard. Here's a sample of what your template could look like using my virtues list from Chapter 8.

Date _____	1	2	3	4	5
Industry					
Minimize timewasters (e.g., unnecessary meetings, "pick your brain" lunches, junk TV, etc.).					
Follow-through on promises/deadlines.					
Avoid procrastination.					
Notes:					
Positivity					
Make time for inspirational reading.					
Catch and release attack thoughts.					
Practice forgiveness.					
Disengage in littleness or gossip.					
Notes:					

	1	2	3	4	5
Career Goal: Host a Lunch 'n Learn on social media.					
Notes:					
Career Goal: Write feature for April newsletter on Expo committee.					
Notes:					

By the way, a huge clue that you're truly changing your habits is when you find yourself actually wanting to engage in this practice. It won't feel like "one more thing" on a long list of "things" to accomplish each day. It will become a gift to yourself and, over time, the intentions on your score sheets will no longer feel like "exercises." Many of them will become rituals, as much a part of your day as getting out of bed and brushing your teeth—and that's the idea. If there ever comes a point in your career where you don't feel you are "getting" enough out of it, be honest about how much you're giving. Are you really *doing* or just wanting and trying?

P.S. Now that you've seen how well you stack up against your own success profile, fast-forward to "Section 6: Toolbox" and use the personal career assessment (Tool 3) to see how well you do against your company's own recruiting profile.

CHAPTER TEN

six ways to earn respect under the corporate umbrella...

and seven ways to screw it up royally

Never bend your head. Always hold it high. Look the world straight in the eye.
—Helen Keller

HAVING WORKED IN both small businesses and corporate environments, I can tell you there's a huge difference between the two. Small businesses typically have more wildfire cultures where everyone is expected to do 20 things at once, such as write the proposal, bind the doc, package it, *and* call FedEx to pick it up at the same time. There's no such thing as flying under the radar, and if you don't have the answer, well, you figure it out.

I learned this lesson firsthand just a few months into my career while working for a small business where one of my first jobs was to help our team manage a large conference. On the day of the event itself, I watched in mild amusement as our team leader, I'll call her Brenda, strapped on *roller skates*—yes, roller skates—to make speedy trips from building to building. Small-business employees reading this may not agree with the tactic but will certainly recognize the scrappy ingenuity you have to display when things need to get done and there's no extra money or help to do them. And while I have to tip my hat to Brenda's creativity, I can tell you that she wouldn't have lasted long in corporate life.

That's because big business is more of a controlled, slow burn. This isn't to say things don't get busy (ha!), only that it's easier to shuffle the ball under the coconut . . . to find *someone else* to mail the package—and to blame that person if it doesn't arrive on time. In large organizations, there are usually lead characters and supporting cast. The stars themselves can't hide, of course, but their shadow is often broad enough that others can take cover.

Small Business versus Large Organizations: Two Different Cultures, Two Different Games

When I transitioned from a series of small-business employers to a corporate position, it was like sliding into a pair of skinny jeans. Tight, yet oddly comfortable. I loved the fact that my coworkers used terms like *v1* (translation: the first draft), *processing in real time* (translation: thinking out loud), and *under development* (translation: this task is totally behind). I had a courier service, mileage reimbursement (without the guilt at least), two monitors, and a personal conference call line. It was awesome. Still, I quickly realized there were some unspoken rules of the game for anyone making the move to corporate life.

Six Ways to Earn Respect Under the Corporate Umbrella

1. *Pay attention to your title.* A few years ago, the accounting firm I worked for was merging with a much larger company. Naturally, there were a million and one details that went along with this transaction, from ordering signage and stationery to informing clients and media, combining records, introducing staff . . . the list was overwhelming. Still, there was one "tiny" detail that caused major gridlock: the org chart. *"You've never seen anything like it,"* said one of the partners. *"Everyone was absolutely consumed with where they fell on that document."* At the time I remember thinking this reaction was over-the-top and totally egotistical. In my small biz role, no one had the luxury of worrying about pecking order, which would have been ridiculous anyway, because there were so few of us. I've since learned that in the corporate space your title and position really do matter . . . *a lot.* Right or wrong, it's how other people judge your value to the organization, which, right or wrong, does make a difference in how they treat you. That's why I hate it when I hear women say things like, *"I don't need a fancy title—I just want to be known as the person who gets the job done."* Bullshit. You need both.

2. *Know what you're responsible for* now. Before I signed on to join the accounting firm, I met with the managing partner for breakfast. A week earlier he had sent me an e-mail saying that if I ever wanted to leave the small marketing agency I worked for, he had a "nice, cushy job" waiting. He wasn't kidding. The hostess had barely seated us before he was offering me a new position at double my current salary.

"What would I be doing?" I asked.

"Marketing," he said.

"*Great*," I replied. "*So what does that mean? What are the responsibilities of the job?*"

He didn't know. It was a new position and everything was still up in the air. While I was still wildly tempted to scream "*Yes!*" and jump out of my chair with a celebratory fist-pump, I kept my cool and accepted the offer under one condition: I had to have a job description. At the time, my chief concern was that "marketing" could be secret code for "admin" and I'd wind up being his de facto executive assistant. I wanted to protect myself by making sure that we were on the same page about *what* I was responsible for (and what I wasn't), *who* I would report to, and *how* my success would be measured. This was—without question—one of the best decisions I've ever made in my career.

If you don't have a job description in place right now, don't wait until your performance review—bring it up with your supervisor ASAP. (Yes, even if you've been in your position for years.) Assuming you want to move up, you need to be clear on *precisely* what your current role is so that you can make a case for a promotion when you've mastered it. Make sense? Likewise, never accept a new position—even an internal one—without getting your responsibilities and reporting structure in writing. Better to be smart now than sorry later.

3. *Know what you want next.* Recently I met a program manager at Microsoft who has managed to make herself reDONKulously valuable in a short amount of time. First, she spearheaded a high-profile volunteer project for the company—and masterfully promoted it by getting senior leaders to write about it on their blogs. Then, to capitalize on her increased visibility, she created a 15-slide "Career Development Plan" PowerPoint that outlined her values, passions, achievements, competencies, and future goals and provided testimonials from other employees who had worked with her. She said she regularly sends the doc to execs within Microsoft with an invitation for a brief chat. To date, she has never been turned down. But more than that, her development plan initially outlined her desire to move to the United States from her native Australia and—you guessed it—she is now enjoying the view from her new office outside Seattle.

"*All I had to do was prove myself, then make it clear what I wanted,*" she said, "*and things started lining up for me in that direction.*" Amen, sister.

4. *Watch your image.* In the corporate world, you are expected to look the part. So look the part because when your appearance is a wreck people automatically assume your whole life is a wreck.

5. *Keep the "confidential" confidential.* While serving as marketing director for the accounting firm, I found myself responsible for the logistics of our big merger announcement. Imagine the scene: You show up in the morning on what you think will be a routine work day only to find a series of trolley cars outside your office. You and all of your colleagues aren't given any information other than to jump onboard. Then everyone is driven to a nearby auditorium. Next thing you know—surprise!—your firm has a new name and—surprise!—you now have new offices throughout the southeastern United States and—surprise!—your career track looks totally different. (Yeah, that's really how it went down.)

As you can guess, it took a ton of moving parts to make this happen without tipping anyone off, and the fact that I was able to quietly work on the project without any I-know-something-you-don't-know hints to colleagues scored major points with my boss. Coming from a small-business environment where *everyone* knew even the tiniest details about *everything*, I learned the importance of discretion within large companies. Our merger—which had been in the works for months—was emphatically denied right up until the point we made the announcement. This wasn't about duping people—it was about controlling the message. And to earn trust, you have be someone who can do that well.

6. *Have patience with the process.* I worked in my first job out of college for exactly two and a half weeks before I was promoted. One day, while casually passing my boss in the hallway, she stopped me and said, *"You have a degree, right?"* I said I did and that was that. Poof! I was the new account coordinator.

But things don't typically go down like that in corporate environments. When you're hired, you're usually in your position for at least a year before you would even be considered to move up. I once interviewed a young woman within a Fortune 50 organization who said she was frustrated with her career path because she was in a position that had a two-year promotion track. *"Two years is like a decade to me,"* were her exact words. I had to laugh at that . . . but I get it. When you're ambitious, it's frustrating to appear powerless over the timing of your own success. Not to mention, it's easy to feel as if you're falling behind when we're all surrounded by tales of 27-year-old CEOs.

That said, any decision made out of impatience usually turns out to be the wrong one—especially major career decisions. This doesn't mean you should become complacent by any stretch, but it does mean that you should have a modicum of respect for the established protocols within your organization and be willing—again—to see the bigger picture. There are a lot of circumstances around a promotion that you may not be privy to just yet. For example, if you are a new grad and were hired in a wave of other new grads, how would it look to everyone else if *you* were promoted in six months? Even if you deserve it, there still needs to be a plan in place for how managers will handle inquiries from everyone else wondering when it's going to be their turn. Get it? It's not just about you.

Seven Ways to Royally Screw Up Your Reputation

1. *Making stupid excuses.* "*But no one told me . . . But I never received any guidance . . . But no one got back to me.*" Ugh . . . work victims suck. If you don't have answers, *ask questions.* Ask for clarifications up front and feedback along the way, and be open to any and all critiques without getting your undies in a bind. Maybe even turn in a rough version of whatever you are working on to your supervisor *while it's in progress* to see if you're on the right track. Then check in, asking questions like, "*How am I doing? Does this meet your expectations? Is there anything I can improve upon?*" You don't want to bird-dog your boss or clients to the point of annoyance, but you do want to get answers on the front end so you don't have to make lame "*but I didn't know how*" excuses on the back end.

2. *Missing deadlines.* If you want to earn respect, be the person who doesn't need an e-mail reminder to get your work done. That means if the deadline is on the 24th of the month, you deliver by 5:00 p.m. on the 24th, not before midnight on the 25th or—worse—after the client e-mails you to see what's up.

3. *Poor meeting prep.* Can we all quit sending review docs and slide decks 60 seconds before the meeting starts? Thanks.

4. *Being tit-for-tat on time and money.* I once had a manager tell me of an employee who had a 5:00 p.m. flight to a regional sales meeting. Since the flight was two hours long, she figured her workday would end around 7:00 p.m. Therefore, she felt completely justified in her request to show up that morning at 10:30 a.m.—not because she had something important to handle, mind you, but because she considered anything past 5:00 p.m. overtime and, even though she was salaried, she thought the company owed her those two hours. Now . . . this is a person who worked in a showroom where *anyone's* absence meant the rest of the team had to work harder to pick up the slack. So here's how the story ends: Not only did her manager flatly deny her request to come in late but—in that instant—any leadership equity she had built with him was damaged. (Note: If you can't see a thing wrong with the employee's request, you're probably reading the wrong book.)

To be clear, I'm not telling you that regular 60+ hour workweeks with no added compensation from the company (a promotion, raise, extra vacation hours, or even all three) is acceptable. It's not. You have a life. But I am saying that—as with everything else—you have to *give to get*. If you want to advance in your career, you have to see beyond what's most convenient for you at any given time and consider what's best for your team and the company overall. This also goes for turning in an expense report *every single time* you pay a toll or buy a stamp. Yes, that $1.65 is owed to you, but it's another one of those "little" things that scream *I'm-only-here-because-you-pay-me*. If you have a worthy report, by all means file to be reimbursed. But if you just spotted the client a coffee last month and that's all—let it go.

5. *Unresponsiveness.* Good grief, people—ignored e-mail does not mean "no." It only means the sender has to wonder if her e-mail is in your junk folder, if you haven't made a decision yet, or if you're just avoiding her. Either way, it's rude. Obviously, this advice doesn't apply to messages where you're cc'd or messages that don't require a direct response; even so, if someone has taken the time to reach out to you personally, for Pete's sake respect the person enough to respond—even if your answer isn't what she wants to hear.

6. *Being the center of your own jokes.* Self-deprecating humor is exactly that. Self-deprecating. It makes you small. When you tell a joke at your own expense—about your weight, your abilities, your "blonde moments," whatever—you may think it's harmless or that you're just having fun. Nope. What you're really doing is affirming that negative perception in your own mind and in the mind of others. That's because every thought you think and word you say has energy attached to it. High-level thoughts and words have high-level energy while—you guessed it—low-level thoughts and words have low energy. Each will become like a magnet in your life.

In order for others to respect you, you have to respect yourself first. If that's too "woo-woo" for you, just remember my friend "Amy." (And, no, that's not her real name.) Early in her career while trying to be "one of the girls," Amy made a joke about meeting up with her boyfriend for a red-hot lunch special (yeah, it's what you think it is). That tryst earned her the nickname "nooner," which, unfortunately, spread like wildfire through the office gossip channels. Poor Amy. What started as a tiny joke ended up putting a sizable dent in her reputation at work.

But before you accuse me of being the mean headmistress, I should point out that—yes, I'm very aware that a robust sense of humor is required to survive in business. (Perhaps now more than ever.) That said, it's one thing to know how to take or tell a joke, and something entirely different to "make" yourself a joke. When you turn yourself into a punching bag, you are subtly giving others permission to do the same.

7. *Missing the small stuff.* Think details don't matter? Tell that to the graduates of the University of Texas Lyndon B. Johnson "School of Pubic Affairs." Whoever let *that* typo appear on the commencement booklet—true story—has certainly learned the, um, hard way that "little" things are actually quite big.

woman 2 woman: Owning Your Career
"Your reputation is everything. You build your personal brand through everything you do, whether big actions or small decisions, and that brand will stay with you throughout your career. So choose to build it positively by dressing appropriately, taking the high road in office politics, supporting the development of others, volunteering for

projects, and adding value wherever you can. Also, remember to have patience—you're building the foundation for a lifelong career. In the beginning, I didn't realize the skills and lessons I was learning at that time would be invaluable in the future. I simply wanted to hurry it all up. I know now that it's like building a house: The stronger the foundation, the higher you can go."

—Jan Fields, president, McDonald's USA

"I have worked in 10 different departments and held 15 different titles during my two decades at Mylan. As a result, I feel like I know the organization inside and out. But one of the drawbacks of my career path is that I sometimes felt overlooked as someone who could play a critical role. Instead, the company sought to bring in 'experts' from the outside with better perceived experience. My advice to anyone—this doesn't just apply to women—is to seek out and ask for opportunities in different departments or in areas that are outside your comfort zone. Don't wait for someone to ask you—they might not think to do so. Growth is not necessarily in a straight line, and developing a broader set of skills and a knowledge base by volunteering for a position in a new area will open you up to far more opportunities down the road."

—Heather Bresch, CEO, Mylan

CHAPTER ELEVEN

a note to new grads

ONE OF THE FIRST questions on the executive women's survey for this book was, *"In your current or most recent position, do you work with or hire college grads?"* The question didn't ask respondents to distinguish between male and female grads, which is important to note because, frankly, the results weren't all that great. Here's what they said:

> **While 68 percent of respondents work with or hire new grads, only 26 percent felt those grads were pre-pared for the realities and demands of the workforce.**

Blimey.

Roughly three-quarters of the 700+ executives who took the survey don't believe the new class is cutting it. Moreover, this question obviously struck a chord because almost half of the survey participants left a comment on it. I'll start with the positives.

There's no doubt employers understand new grads are incredibly tech-savvy, have a spectacular ability to multitask, and bring a lot of energy and enthusiasm to their jobs. But here's where it gets dicey. Out of the 328 comments on this question, a full one-third of respondents *specifically* mentioned they believed new grads felt "entitled" to rewards they hadn't earned yet and otherwise demonstrated a low work ethic.

Okay, so it's already extraordinary that—on this survey at least—almost three-quarters of women executives don't believe new hires are well prepared for the workforce, but it's *doubly* shocking that so many of the folks who left comments listed work ethic as the primary cause.

So . . . this is the part where you (and I mean everyone, not just new grads) need to get honest about whether you are putting in the time and displaying the commitment required to counter feedback such as this and really succeed in your field.

Let's slice this data up a little bit more. Here's what survey respondents said when asked, "*Of the following four choices, which skill do you feel is most lacking in new grad hires?*"

Communication skills	30 percent
Critical thinking and problem solving	27 percent
Taking initiative	25 percent
Follow-through	18 percent

Must-Have Skill #1: Communication

Question to ask yourself: How good are you at connecting with other people?

Since some studies show that up to 93 percent of communication is nonverbal, the ability to "read" others and get a sense of what's going on *behind* their words is critically important. That said, the fact that we use technology to communicate essentially *everything* these days is resulting in a slow erosion of this critical skill. In fact, neurologists are discovering that the younger their study participants, the less likely they are to recognize common facial cues.

Maybe this finding doesn't come as much of a surprise to you, given the epic interpersonal failures we've all heard about or experienced firsthand. Still, if you work with someone (or lots of someones) and they just don't seem to "get it"—it could be because they do the majority of their communicating online. (Oh, and perhaps it's also because we're all so saturated with reality TV, which showcases the worst of how to communicate, but that's another book.)

While there's plenty on resolving conflict in Chapter 14, "Solve the Freakin Problem!" I do have one additional note on this subject:

E-mail is *not* your medium for resolving a disagreement—so stop!

When I tell people this, it never fails: I always have someone who says something like, *"Well, I'd rather use e-mail when I'm mad because then I can say exactly what I want and the other person won't see me upset."*

While that's true, here's the problem: After you've hit SEND and *you* feel good, there's no way of knowing how the other person is going to react. The person may take your message the wrong way, which will make the situation ten times worse than it could have been. Remember: Whatever message you think you're sending means nothing compared to the one that is received. If you are looking to build real, no-fluff relationships with the people you work with, remember, that's *always* a face-to-face game.

Must-Have Skill #2: Critical Thinking and Problem Solving

Question to ask yourself: Am I an idea generator, or do I just look things up?

There's no doubt "growing up Google" has been extraordinary. Whereas previous employees were forced to hunt through outdated manuals, pound the stairs at the library, and—OMG—*wait for* the material they wanted, we now have answers to any question you can imagine delivered piping hot in less than a second. Believe me, I'm not romanticizing the "way it was before." I don't want to go back there, either. But the truth is, we've become addicted to immediacy, and it has not only impacted our ability to generate new ideas, it has also meant we expect every question in business to have a black-and-white answer.

For example, let's say you're chugging along at work and—oops!—you accidentally make one of your company's largest clients very angry. What now? What's the Google search for *"I f*cked up big time"*? Sure, you could plug that in your search engine and—after you've waded through all the porn—there may be some nuggets of valuable business advice. But none will cover the very real nuances of your situation.

So, as you are attempting to build a name for yourself at work, it's important to note that you will go further, faster if you can assure your boss and colleagues that not only are you an employee who doesn't expect solutions to be spoon-fed or found online, but you can come up with solid ideas on your own.

woman 2 woman:
Get the Job Before You Get the Job

"Fresh out of Purdue University and seemingly a world away from my hometown of Abingdon, Illinois—population 3,500 or so—I took my first job working for the accounting firm of Arthur Andersen & Co. in Chicago.

"Talk about a culture shock.

"It wasn't just that I was barely out of the classroom and suddenly in the middle of the Big City. I was also the very first woman professional that Arthur Andersen [and] Andersen Consulting—now known as Accenture—had ever hired. I was, as some of my colleagues back then in the mid-1960s didn't hesitate to say, an "*Andersen man in a skirt.*"

"As a new grad and a woman, I found the most important thing I needed to do was learn my way around. I began with something very simple: lunch. Each day, I would eat by myself in the cafe while the men would talk about sports and clients and whatever else they talked about. I didn't want to impose on their conversations, so I waited for them to invite me to join them. Problem was, that didn't happen. After a while, I just invited myself.

"It became a good networking opportunity and a way to learn more about my coworkers, about my company, and about my eventual pathway to the top of the corporate ladder. I learned that if I was going to move up the ranks, I needed to start planning my ascent. So I began to ask myself what I would be doing next year, in three years, in five years. I began setting goals.

At the time, I was in the consulting business, so I was assigned to client projects. And like any bright-eyed recent graduate, I assumed that if I did my projects in an outstanding way, I would get promoted accordingly—and in keeping with the grand plans I had set for myself. But that didn't just happen, either.

"What I came to realize was that, even though I had set goals for my next job, I had to actually *perform* the job I wanted before I would get promoted to it. I eventually figured out that—even though I was young and new—if I wanted to be promoted to a manager in the future, I had to perform like a manager *in the moment*. And in order to perform like a manager, I had to build and demonstrate the skills, the capabilities, and experience to move up. I also learned that I needed to package myself as a manager. I needed to act the part and I needed others to perceive me as if I were already a manager. I realized then that I needed to take responsibility for who I was and what I wanted to be. If I didn't, who would? I decided I would have to manage my career like a business if I wanted to make it in the business world. So, in addition to setting aside time for strategic planning and setting goals, I built a team of advisers, advocates, and mentors—like a business would have a board of directors—to help guide me on my way.

"As part of my strategic career plan, I decided that I wanted to be perceived as if I were in Accenture for the long haul. When I did, the opportunities kept opening for me. People were willing to invest in me and my career. Fourteen years after becoming the first female professional at Arthur Andersen, I was named the first female partner of its consulting organization, Andersen Consulting. I later became the managing partner for Accenture's office of the CEO, and then went on to serve on Accenture's executive committee and as president of the Accenture Foundation.

"All of this happened because, fresh out of college, I decided I needed to set my career goals, ask for what I wanted, and make things happen for me, not let things happen to me. In essence, I was the CEO of Me, Inc. You should be that, too."

—Susan Bulkeley Butler, CEO of the
Susan Bulkeley Butler Institute for
the Development of Women Leaders

.... *SECTION 3 ROUNDUP* ....
How to Handle: Tricky Service Situations @ Work
....

When: You're not productive or are constantly running behind.

You Should: *Get strategic about your day.* With the advent of social media, "killing time" on the job has never been easier. Unfortunately, neither has killing your credibility. In *Effective*

Immediately, Skip and I wrote about the importance of having a Power Hour every day—that one thin slice of uninterrupted time where you can truly focus on *the work*, not all of the meetings and noise surrounding it. One solid hour is enough for many execs; however, if you still feel like you need a more structured routine, try day-blocking. Here's a sample of what a day-blocked schedule might look like for a typical office worker:

Day-Blocking

Wake to 9:00 a.m.—A hybrid of "you" time and "work" time. Ideally, this is the window where you'd get your inspirational reading in, your exercise on, and respond to any e-mails from the night before.

9:00 a.m. to noon—All "you" time. In other words, your e-mail is closed (that's right—closed), you don't sneak to see who retweeted you, you don't text your sweetie, and you don't schedule any phone calls or meetings. I know, I know—this won't always be possible. The point is not to schedule anything for yourself here *if you can help it*. Be flexible when you have to. Otherwise, reserve this precious three-hour window for banging out items from your to-do list, starting with the highest-priority item and working down without distraction.

Noon to 12:30 p.m.—Lunchtime. Yes, you're slammed, but everyone has to eat. Take your lunch, people.

12:30 to 5:30 p.m.—All "them" time. You are now at the disposal of your team and free to provide feedback, schedule calls, attend meetings, and get to the coveted finish line for every professional: inbox zero. One small caveat, though: At the end of the day, before you shut down and go home, take a few minutes to review what you've accomplished and create your to-do list for tomorrow.

Everything you need to know about productivity is here in day-blocking, but if you are already thinking your job would never allow you to adopt this schedule, you're right. Your job won't, so it has to come from you. Once you get into the habit of respecting your own time, you'll discover that you can actually train other people to respect it, too.

When: You want to get noticed super fast.

You Should: *Become insanely useful.* You can start by looking for the pebble in the shoe of your supervisor. Where can she use help? Make that your "silver bullet"—the place where you add enormous value. (Hint: One area where companies seem to need a lot of help these days is writing.) You'll also get noticed if you can find clever ways to save the company money without scrimping on service. Warning: Whatever you raise your hand for, make sure it weighs heavier on the strategic side vs. the administrative. If your supervisor's pebble is working the A/V in the conference room, you can become the go-to person alright, but it won't help you much in your long-term career pursuit.

When: You really want to impress a client.

You Should: *Listen.* A great manager of mine once said, "*Every client wants two things: solutions to their problems and warm fuzzies.*" In other words, regardless of whether your clients are internal or external, they want the job done right, and they want to feel good about selecting you to do it. That's all.

The problem is, too often we assume we already know what clients want. So we smack the horse on the ass and start running full gallop (*"Hi-YA!"*) into what we think is the right direction. But is it?

If you want to impress clients—and I mean *really* impress them—take time on the front end to listen. This, of course, means you have to ask the right questions first, so here's a few to get you started.

1. What's at the top of your mind today? Is there anything besides what I have listed on the agenda that you'd like to talk about? (After the usual round of small talk and chit-chat, you should begin every client interaction with some form of this critically important, yet often-overlooked, question.)

2. What are your biggest challenges right now?

3. What's working out well?

4. What would make this experience/project the best possible for you?

5. What would make it a waste of your time?

6. On a scale of 1 to 10, with 10 being exceptional, what could I or my team do to earn a 10?

7. If budget or time were no object, what would you do?

8. Is there anything you'd like to cover that we haven't discussed?

Resist the ever-present temptation to run before you walk by getting clear on the client's success metrics first.

When: Your client asks for something way outside your agreed-upon scope of work. (It's worth noting that while they may play dumb, most clients know exactly what they're doing here.)

You Should: *Revisit your original agreement.* This is always a tricky situation. On one hand, it's great news. Yay—more business! (More on that in a moment.) On the other hand, the client may expect you to handle the job at no extra charge. Boo—more business.

The solution is to gently point your client back to the initial agreement where—ahem—expectations and deadlines should be always be clearly defined. This is why we have agreements in the first place, right? So your response could go something like this: *"Tom, thanks for the opportunity to work on this project for you. I'm sure we can take care of it. Let me do some initial research and if it looks like it's going to require a fair amount of time, I'll be happy to work up a price and get back to you. Does that sound good?"*

Make sure any additional work is listed as an addendum to your contract—and get the client to re-sign. This step will not only protect your company, but it also sends a message to the client that you have a low tolerance for scope creep.

As a rule, more business is a good thing. I know that sounds obvious, but you will inevitably have colleagues who don't think so. They'll bark at new jobs, claim to be overextended already, and whine about their full schedules. Don't take the bait. If you need help, build a solid case for it with your boss. If not, don't jump on the pity parade. *Take every opportunity to do additional work for your clients.* It's much easier to keep current customers happy than it is to find new ones (which is great for your company), but when clients are raving about you—all of a sudden you become extremely valuable. Hello, leverage!

When: Your client begins to nickel-and-dime over everything.

You Should: *Reassess your value.* It's a serious red flag when clients start nitpicking invoices, because it means they are questioning the *value* you provide. So instead of asking them to go line-by-line on PO#3876 (snooze), try picking up the phone instead and saying: *"Nicole, I got your e-mail about the invoice. Is this a good time for a quick chat?"* If the client agrees, you want to start with the very big picture. *"I just wanted to touch base for a moment and talk to you about our service in general. On a scale of 1 to 5, with 1 being outstanding, how are we doing on this end? Please be perfectly honest."*

Reality check time: Don't expect her to give you a 1. Assuming your invoice reflects the rate Nicole signed off on at the beginning of the job, the pricing wouldn't be an issue unless she felt a lack of return. Therefore, use this opportunity to push her for improvement areas. For example, ask: *"What would a rating of 1 look like to you?"* Don't try to defend your firm at this point; don't say for example, *"Well, as you know, that project was late because your assistant didn't send us the files on time."* Instead, just listen and take really good notes. Depending on the severity of the issues, you can decide whether to handle it yourself, alert your team, or go straight to your boss.

Also, if you are not already involved with the invoicing process, it's a good idea to inject yourself—if only for a once-over before the bill is sent to the client. That way you can ensure all items listed are accurate and there's no vague "miscellaneous" charges to attract further scrutiny. Even if the client is cool through the process and the inquiry turns out to be a nonissue, you still need to take it as a signal that this client needs more solutions and warm fuzzies. For example, if you've been slacking on the Friday Updates (See Chapter 7), now's a perfect time to get disciplined and get those out each week. The bottom line is: *Never assume clients know how hard you're working for them.*

Finally, remember your work is most valuable to clients the moment it's delivered. So make sure your invoices are going out on time!

When: Your clients always want their work yesterday.

You Should: *Accommodate sparingly.* When I worked in advertising, we had a statement prepared for addressing this type of client: *"You can have your work cheap, fast, or good. Pick two."* Believe me—I know you want to do everything possible to help your client in a pinch, but it can't always be at the expense of your office morale. So, before you promise any rush job to a client—STOP!—and consider one question: *Is this due date realistic for the team, given our bandwidth right now?*

It's common to assume projects will take less time than they actually do or to believe clients when they say it'll "just take a few minutes." (As if.) To handle these sticky situations, consider creating (or asking for) a few guidelines on how long your organization's core services usually take, so you have some idea when discussing those items with your clients.

For example, if you work for a marketing firm and you have an "at-a-glance" reference that says brochures take 21 business days . . . you're probably not going to promise the client you can turn one around in 10 days. However, if you don't have those guidelines, you may delude yourself into believing 10 days is not only possible, but could even be reasonable. (More on the topic of work plans in a moment.) Meanwhile, back at the ranch, this schedule will cause major tension as designers and copywriters have to shuffle *their* projects to accommodate your big mouth. Not good. So tell your client, *"I'd love to help you with that. Let me check in with our team to make sure they are able to meet your deadline, though, because I don't want to overpromise on our end and risk disappointing you."*

Look, everyone knows rush work happens. It's part of business, and there will definitely be times where it's your job to make the project work regardless of who's inconvenienced. At this point you can actually get away with it *because* (keyword alert) it doesn't happen all the time.

That said, you have to set some ground rules with clients— even the seemingly innocuous, well-intentioned ones. A diplomatic push back isn't a sign of bad service—but rest assured, under-delivering is. Checking in with your team first on rush jobs is not only the courteous thing to do, but it's also in the best interest of your clients. Don't forget—they're making plans on their end, too. If you caved and promised that brochure in ten days and the client turns around and sends an e-blast to its clients telling them to "check their mailboxes" in a week, you're beyond screwed and worse off than if you had just said "no" in the first place. (Also, consider this: Once you've demonstrated your capacity to deliver on a rush job, you may have trouble getting clients back on normal scheduling. Therefore, don't make it too easy for them to get their work yesterday. Like, ever.)

Since we're on the topic of work plans, be sure to build in a few days to marinate on the finished product before you deliver it. (Yes, I can feel you glaring at me through the page. You're thinking, *"HA! If only, Bennington!"*) Like most people, if a project is due on the 28th, you're not only still working on the 28th, but you're hoping to deliver by 12:00 a.m. (After all, anything before midnight still counts, right?) Well . . . here's the problem with that. Often, the difference between "good" and "wow" happens in that space *after* a project is "finished" but *before* it goes to the client. In other words, it's that unrushed period of time when you can read through it without the pressure to immediately attach it to an e-mail, hit "SEND," then collapse in your chair. It's that space where you can run the numbers again. Where you can catch bad grammar. Where you can actually show it to someone else for input—*and* give them more than three minutes to review. Most of the time, we don't ever get to this point. We pass work off as "good enough" and move on to the next job. But do you really think you'll move up for being "good enough?"

When: Your client is nuclear pissed.

You Should: *Respond ASAP.* Uh-oh. Maybe you've run into a massive project delay, hit a five-figure budget overrun, or the solution you pitched your client has simply become unattainable. Suffice it to say, you've *really* stepped in it this time. Well . . . the good news is that in business, you always have two opportunities to make a great impression: when you meet someone new and when you screw up.

A few years ago, I worked for a manager who had a great formula for overcoming surprises and maintaining a client's trust. His solution was to respond ASAP.

"A" = Apologize. Tell your client that you made a mistake honestly and immediately. Don't leave out or sugarcoat important details; just inform the client as soon as you become aware of the problem. For example, *"Chris, something has come up. I've just learned that our development group has to recode one whole section of the software. On behalf of our team, I apologize for this unexpected news, but I want you to know we are researching multiple solutions and we will get this resolved for you."*

"S" = Sympathize. The fastest way to drive a wedge between you and your clients is if they think you don't care. So take the extra time to let them know how terrible you feel about the situation. This is your opportunity to do a lot of sincere listening (and less talking) because they'll probably want to vent a bit. Simply let them have their say and respond with genuine concern: *"Chris, I know that you don't like surprises, and I completely understand that you are disappointed. I felt exactly the same when I learned about this."*

"A" = Action Plan. This is the part where you let the client know—in a very straightforward manner—how you plan to remedy the situation. Ideally, you would be able to so in person, but if that's not possible, a phone or video conference call is the next best thing. Don't lean too heavily on e-mail here. If the client is angry or severely inconvenienced (or both), you need to actually hear and respond to the unfiltered language and tone. Also, this is not the time to stare blankly and expect the client to decide what to do next. This is the time to show up having done your homework on possible resolutions, and be willing to discuss them all, while ready to champion one. The goal—as always—is to become a true strategic partner in your client's business, and that won't happen if you need the client to take over when things get tough while you run around like your hair's on fire. Trying saying something like this: *"We believe we have the trouble area identified and we are going to work overtime to get it straightened out. The quality control team is prepared to expedite the project when it comes through. Worst case, we are looking at a two-month delay here, but with some luck, we can make it up somewhere in the final phase."*

"P" = Perform. Show time! Your reputation is on the line here and this is a pivotal juncture in your client relationship. Depending on how you handle the situation, if you and your team recover well, the client will be satisfied and possibly even impressed. Who knows—your snafu could actually bring you closer. (Well, assuming you don't screw up too often.)

When: Your client wants to hire you.

You Should: *Proceed with caution.* Ideally, here's how this process is *supposed* to work: The client, after being blown away by your stellar service, decides you would be a great fit for his team. Subsequently, the client's first call would be to your boss—not you—to clue her in. This may seem unfair—after all, it is *your* career on the line—but when there's a business relationship at stake, reaching out to your manager first is considered proper protocol. Once aware of the client's intentions, your boss then gives him the green light to contact to you directly.

Now, you are in the enviable position of having a choice between the client's offer or a revised compensation package from your boss, who will no doubt try to up the ante to keep you onboard. *Yay you, right?*

Here's where it gets squirrelly. If the client bypasses your boss and contacts you directly, what are you supposed to do then? If you enter into negotiations behind your boss's back, then announce you're quitting, she will no doubt feel betrayed by you and the client, setting the stage for a seriously awkward departure at minimum and a burned bridge at worst.

So, assuming you are interested in discussing the client's offer further, the next thing out of your mouth after *"Thank you for the opportunity"* should be, *"Have you spoken to my supervisor about this?"* If the answer is "yes," you're covered. If it's "no," you owe it to your current employer to bring her into the loop. This is obviously not something you want to send over e-mail, so schedule a few minutes with your boss to speak to her directly. Game tip: Have a clear idea of the client's official offer before you go into any meeting. You don't want to stir the pot if the client isn't 100 percent serious. (You only make decisions on facts, remember?)

Now, if you're clawing at the walls to leave and there's nothing your boss could say or do to get you to stay, then you can take a courteous but more decisive approach. For instance, *"Tanea, I spoke to Jeff today and he has asked me to join his team as a sales manager. I wanted to be honest and up front with you, because I'm giving it very serious consideration."*

However, if you're on the fence and want to use the client's offer as leverage for a raise or other perks, you should know what you want before meeting with your boss. Assuming you're a valued employee, she will most likely ask if there's anything the company can do to keep you. Obviously, this is not the time to stutter incoherently and say you'll give it some thought. It's the time to speak up and get what you want. For example, state that *"Jeff is offering to give me ownership of projects with a budget range of $200,000 to $250,000, which is appealing because I feel ready to work on larger accounts."*

Another game tip: Lead with the work first. This is a terrific opportunity to bargain for more authority (note I didn't say responsibility), but you don't want your boss to think money is the only factor in your decision. If you genuinely want to stay, you need her to understand that you care about your future with the company—and kicking off the discussion with a salary ultimatum doesn't quite send that message.

If you and your boss agree to some general terms related to your job function, now's the time to talk turkey. Again, the key is to come into the discussion knowing what you want. For example: *"Jeff is offering a salary that is 10 percent more than my base here, plus an additional three days of vacation. Is that an offer you would be willing to match?"*

Most likely you won't get a decision on the spot and—when you do receive word—it won't be everything you asked for. So, as with any successful negotiation, always know what your minimum requirements are and be willing to walk away if necessary. But before you throw down that card, be absolutely certain you are willing to follow through and leave the company. Because if you're bluffing and the boss calls you on it— *"Wow, that's too bad. We're really going to miss you"*—you're going to feel pretty dumb.

One final note: If you have a noncompete agreement with your current employer, that document trumps everything I just said.

Action Plan: Personal Effectiveness Goals

Select three goals from the following table and write them in the career plan template provided as Tool 1 in the Section 6 Toolbox. (For an e-version of the career plan, please visit www.emilybennington .com/templates.)

Action	Points
Create your own VIG list. (See Chapter 8.)	15
Create your VIG practice using Scorecards A and/or B (see Chapter 9).	15
Write your own performance review—regardless of whether your actual review is days, weeks, or even months away. Pretend you are your boss writing a fabulous, glowing assessment of your work. Now, what do you have to do—immediately—to live up to that?	15

Tip: Share the (nongushing) highlights of your self-review with your boss to make sure you're working in line with her expectations.

Day-block for (at least) one month. (See "How to Handle Tricky Service Situations @ Work," for an example of a day-blocked schedule.)	15
Design your own Career Development Plan in Power-Point (or Keynote for Mac users), listing your personal values, passions, achievements, competencies, future goals, and colleagues' testimonials.	15
Originate a new client or new business opportunity with a current client.	15
Step up to lead an internal committee.	15
Have an article published in a regional newspaper or magazine.	15
Join a professional networking group within your industry.	15
Read *Effective Immediately: How to Fit In, Stand Out, and Move Up at Your First Real Job*, by yours truly and Skip Lineberg. Yes, I know I'm biased, but I promise you'll still get a solid crash course in business —even if it's not your first real job.	*15*
Find something around your office that needs improvement (e.g., the filing system, workroom, proposals, etc.) then suggest—and implement, if appropriate—a process to make it more efficient. For example, if your colleagues	15

are always complaining that they have no idea who to
call in which department for what, rather than jump
on their unmerry bandwagon, create a list of extensions.

Before you leave work, create a list of the top five   15
things you want to accomplish the next day, arranged
by priority. Do this every day for at least one month.

Update your calendar with items that consistently need   10
to get done (e.g., send Friday Updates each week) so
that you can calendar-block time for them.

Update your professional bio. Even if your company   10
has someone assigned to do this for you, take responsibility for keeping it in check. Not only will coworkers
around the company use it to research you, but—
especially if you work for a professional services firm—
you need a good bio to be included in proposals. And
since proposals usually showcase the firm's A-team, you
want to be on them.

Create a 100 percent complete LinkedIn profile—not   10
just the skeleton deal where you list only two or three
words for each position. Always assume your coworkers
and potential clients are reading up on you . . . because
they are.

Register for the industry newsletters and publications   10
of your customers' businesses so that you have a better
sense of how to address their needs. Note: Google
Reader is awesome for this. (5 bonus points for sharing
articles your customers would find particularly valuable.)

Start a kudos file or bulletin board of appreciative and/or congratulatory notes and e-mails from coworkers and clients. (This will also be handy for performance reviews.)	10
Attend a professional development seminar or conference.	10
Attend events hosted or sponsored by your clients to show support for their initiatives.	10
Set a Google Alert for yourself, your boss, your company, clients, and competitors.	5
Host a Lunch 'n Learn on a topic that would be of interest to your office.	5
Set up a whiteboard in your office where you track weekly goals. (Side bonus: Others will notice what you're working on, which is not only a conversation starter but could also open the door for collaboration opportunities.)	5

Section 4:
TEAM DEVELOPMENT

1	2	3	4	5
Self-Awareness	Social Skills	Personal Effectiveness	Team Development	Leadership
			↑ You are here.	

Core Principle

You have the ability to draw the best performance from others because you create an environment where all team members have a clear understanding of their responsibilities, the resources needed to be successful, and feel safe to express their opinions.

In this section, you will learn how to:

- Use "nice" as a career advantage.

- Develop specific coaching language for team development situations.

- Diffuse tense, high-pressure discussions.

What Your Coworkers Are Thinking

"Amanda is someone I trust."

CHAPTER TWELVE

women were raised to be nice. so what?

We begin to find and become ourselves when we notice how we are already found, already truly, entirely, wildly, messily, marvelously who we were born to be.
                                                                    —Anne Lamott

IT'S BEEN SAID that men view business as a sport and women view business as a picnic. In other words, men want to win while women want to make sure everyone has a sandwich and a good time. As you may have noticed, women have been repeatedly bashed for this, as if "playing nice" were a pathetic and career-limiting move.

But is it really?

I mean, if there's one thing we should all know by now, it's that managing by power, aggression, and fear only creates a sicko race to the bottom, which—of course—is *fantastic* news for us girls.

Because if ever there was a time when women should absolutely crush it as leaders, it's right now.

The rise of social media, coupled with the fall of some reckless corporate giants, has created a workforce that is savvy, cynical, and doesn't stand for *anything* iron-fisted, closed-door, or homogenized. We want our leaders not only to be transparent but also to earn our respect, and those who manage "the old way" (that is, by authority alone) will be lapped by those who co-innovate from the front line. *Sweeeet, right?* Because while there are some areas where we can (admittedly) miss the mark, leading by co-innovation isn't one of them.

And the reason this is all so gosh darned important to you, dear reader, is because team building is a make-or-break career skill. To be successful in today's workforce, you have to know how to pull the best from other people—and it ain't about authority. (See Chapter 15, "Having Authority Is Like Having a Gun in Your Closet: There If You Need It, but Hopefully You Won't Have to Pull the Trigger.")

I shouldn't have to say this, but I will anyway: Being kind doesn't mean lowering the bar on what you expect from other people. It simply means you don't have to browbeat them to get it. The command-and-control model is dead. Do you hear me? *Dead.* We don't need any more "leaders" with a stick up their ass. We need people who can *ignite*—particularly in corporate offices where everyone is walking around in zombie-like trances doing things because they're being "compliant," not because they're motivated.

Besides, what is more motivating anyway—the team leader who *forces* or the leader who *encourages*? If it's clearly the one who encourages, then how the hell can the solution to our gender-based leadership gap possibly be to make women meaner? Honestly, the next time you're listening to someone wax on about how women need to "get tougher" I want you to take off your shoe and throw it at the person's head. How's that for playing nice?

Don't Use "Nice" to Compensate for a Lack of Confidence!

Confession time: My interest in women's leadership has very humble beginnings . . . dirty Tupperware, to be exact. Years ago, when I started my first director-level job in a very corporate environment, the first time I delegated an assignment to my assistant I was so afraid she wouldn't like me I actually leaned over and cleaned off her desk.

That's right. After a watered-down, very indirect request and moment of silence that truly was awkward, I picked up two bowls of her dried-up Lean Cuisine from lunch and, in my mousiest voice, said, *"Can I take this for you?"*

Was I trying to be nice? Nope. I was intentionally making myself look weak to come off as a peer. This is where "nice" gets misinterpreted at work. Since no one wants to work for an asshole, "nice" by itself is a good thing, right? The problem is when—as I did—you use "nice" to camouflage debilitatingly low confidence. That's when nice becomes a weakness, not before.

At the time I was busing tables for my assistant, I didn't have anywhere near the same level of confidence *giving* assignments that I had when *being given* assignments. This is a massive hurdle for women, especially when you've just been promoted from a junior to a senior-level role, because it requires a shift in thinking from tactical to strategic and, in many cases, from peer-level to supervisor.

If you're having trouble unlocking that mind-shift yourself, try volunteering for a leadership position outside your office. That way, you'll have an opportunity to build your executive muscles "off the clock." Over time, as you become more confident leading and delegating in your community, you'll notice a parallel confidence building in your "real" job, too.

the cure for
fake harmony

100 coaching questions for team leaders

When you learn, teach.

—Maya Angelou

GALLUP HAS reported that 71 percent of American workers are either "not engaged" or "actively disengaged" in their work. *Say wha?* Imagine if less than a third of your team were top performers while the other two-thirds or so just phoned it in. How would you ever get anything done? Fortunately, there is a cure—and it's pretty simple. You have to care (genuinely) about your people. The remedy to disengagement is its opposite—*engagement*. In other words, get to know them beyond the phony surface level conversations like:

"How was your weekend?"

"Great. And yours?"

"Great."

"Glad to hear it. See you later."

A few weeks after I started working with Skip Lineberg, my first boss and *Effective Immediately* coauthor, he scheduled a meeting with me simply to "chat." It was a practice he adopted from when he was a management trainee at General Electric (GE), and he scheduled similar meetings with all his new employees. At the time, I remember coming into the meeting a little nervous (and, frankly, wondering if I was being "reevaluated" for my position), but it was soon clear that the only thing on Skip's agenda was to get to know his staff better. We had a great discussion and—12 years later—I still remember how it felt to have my boss ask me for input and direction.

Skip is the very definition of a coaching leader. Instead of saying *"You did that wrong,"* he would say, *"Let's think about some different ways that could have been handled."* Once, when I got particularly grumpy with my supervisor, Skip pulled me aside afterward and casually—as if he was asking me to pass the ketchup—said, *"Tell me . . . what kind of impression do you think you're making right now?"* His plan was to get me talking so that I could come to my own conclusion about how out of line I had been . . . and it worked. The minute I realized I was acting like a total moron I stopped. Just like that. However, if Skip had said, *"Look, Emily, you're acting like a total moron,"* I probably would have pulled out my boxing gloves.

See the difference? If you want your team members to invest in you, you have to *invest in them*. And, trust me, they will work harder (*way* harder) if they can tell you care about them as people beyond the "fake harmony" that's so prevalent in offices these days. So here are 100 coaching questions to help you engage your team through various work situations. Authentically giving a crap about the answers is up to you.

Getting to Know You Questions

1. Where are you from?

2. Where does your family live?

3. Who hired you?

4. Where did you go to school?

5. Tell me about your past work experience.

6. What have you done in your life that you're especially proud of?

7. What have you done in your life that no one asked you to do?

8. What kind of books do you like to read?

9. What are your favorite business books?

10. What's new? Bring me up to speed on what's happened since the last time we caught up.

Work-Style Questions

11. Tell me about your preferred work style.

12. Describe your ideal work environment/atmosphere. When are you most productive?

13. When are you least productive?

14. How would you describe your approach to problem solving?

15. Would you rather work with data, people, products, or ideas?

16. How do you prepare for meetings?

17. How do you stay organized?

18. How do you keep track of items to follow up on?

19. What is your preferred learning style?

20. How do you prefer that I communicate with you?

21. How do you see yourself best contributing to this team?

22. Who is the best manager you've ever worked for? What did you like about that person?

23. How do you like to be managed?

24. How can I help you be more effective in your work?

Goals and Development Questions

25. What would you like to achieve in your current role here?

26. What do you see as your next step?

27. What are your career goals over the next two to three years?

28. Is there anyone in the company you'd like an introduction to?

29. What are your personal goals outside of work?

30. When working in teams, what type of roles are you usually assigned? Why do you think that is?

31. What would you consider to be your greatest strengths/weaknesses in your position?

32. How are you working to build on your strengths and compensate for your weaknesses?

33. What new skills would you like to learn?

34. Do you need help navigating the learning and development resources available to you here?

35. Are you involved in any community organizations? Do you need help identifying nonprofits to join?

Job/Career Satisfaction Questions

36. What do you like best about your job? What do you like least?

37. What part of your work feels like drudgery?

38. Do you feel you are made aware enough of what's going on in the business and where we're headed?

39. Do you get enough praise and recognition?

40. Have you been rewarded sufficiently for your work here?

41. How do you feel about morale?

42. Is there anything that you're worried about?

43. What would make you want to leave?

44. What can we do (or do more of) to ensure that you stay?

45. What really bugs you about this place?

46. How do you feel about your coworkers? Do you enjoy working with them?

47. Do we function well as a team?

48. How could we function more efficiently as a team?

Operational Questions

49. Do you have a clear understanding of your role and responsibilities?

50. Do you understand my role?

51. Do you understand your colleagues' roles?

52. What is one thing that I can fix to improve operations?

53. Do you feel we have enough structure and policies? Are they too tight, too loose, about right?

54. If you could change one thing in the office, what would it be?

55. If I could give you one thing to help you in your job, what would it be?

Business Development Questions

56. What new services should we consider offering?

57. Are there any customers/markets that we should pursue?

58. How are our services priced? Are they too high, too low, about right?

59. What feedback or comments do you get from customers about doing business with us?

60. How do you envision our growth over the next year? Ten years from now?

61. What is the best thing we could do, in your opinion, to improve our client service?

Questions for Aligning Expectations

62. Do you understand the scope of this project?

63. Do you understand the delivery format?

64. What's your next step on this project?

65. What will you commit to doing in the next few days (or week) to keep this project moving forward?

66. Do you understand the final deadline?

67. How are you prioritizing this project in relation to your other work?

68. Would you like to schedule any check-in meetings with me?

69. Do you foresee any obstacles to delivering your tasks on time?

70. Is there anything you need from any of the other team members to help you complete your part on schedule?

71. Let's take a moment and pretend we failed on this project. I'm talking complete disaster. Now, can we brainstorm a few reasons we crashed and burned so that we can avoid them from the very beginning?

Questions for Coworkers in a Disagreement

72. Fill me in on the facts here. What actually happened that led up to this situation?

73. Can you tell me what was said, specifically, without assigning any meaning or emotion to it?

74. When she said that, what did you hear?

75. What did you like/dislike about that solution?

76. What is the best outcome in your eyes?

77. What is your least favorite resolution?

78. What resources do you need to resolve this issue? Do you need additional time, funds, or support staff, for instance?

79. If you could cut three things from your workday in order to have more time to focus on (name an issue or project), what would they be?

80. On a scale of 1 to 10, how do you think you've handled this situation so far?

81. Other than what you've stated here (e.g., coworker not pulling his weight), are there any other reasons why the project seems to be stalling?

82. How are you feeling about this situation right now?

83. In the future, how would you prefer your coworker to handle a situation like this? Is there anything you would do differently?

84. What kind of relationship would you like to have with your coworker a year from now?

85. Do you think your behaviors are contributing to that outcome?

86. If you were in my shoes, how would you handle this situation?

87. How important is this issue to you on a scale of 1 to 10?

88. Will it matter one year from now?

89. Give me three possible ways we could tackle this situation.

90. Is there anything else we haven't thought of yet?

91. What progress can we shine a light on today?

92. What challenges do we still have?

Questions for Underperformance

93. If you could pick three adjectives for how you'd like your colleagues/clients to describe you, what would they be?

94. Do you think your behavior is reinforcing the impressions you want to make?

95. How do you think your behavior is impacting the team as a whole?

96. Picture your client receiving this (report, proposal, etc.) today. When it pops open on his screen, how do you think he will view it against the benchmark of the expectations we discussed previously?

97. Is there anything going on outside of work that I should be aware of that could be impacting your performance?

98. What have you learned from this situation?

99. How would you like to see me handle this?

100. If you were working as the best possible version of youself, what would you be doing? (Note: The goal here is to get the coachee talking about specific *actions* she would take if working at her full potential. By pos-

ing the question this way, you're getting her to think about her own behaviors, which not only helps generate buy-in but also allows you to turn around and reframe those same behaviors as *expectations* moving forward. Aren't you smart?)

CHAPTER FOURTEEN

solve the freakin problem!

If you allow yourself to breathe into the depth, wonder, beauty, craziness, and strife—everything that represents fullness in your life—you can live fearlessly. Because you come to realize that if you can just keep breathing, you cannot be conquered.

—Oprah

THE WORKPLACE is full of complex problems and, the higher you go, the more complex they get. Accordingly, one of the biggest factors that separates promotable execs from the "Oh-*hell*-nos" is the ability to diffuse a tense situation rather than escalate it. If you look at where women are supposedly getting it wrong—see Chapter 5, "Indirect, Emotions, and Tears (Oh, My!)"—these aren't the things that happen when life is going just peachy. They happen when everything is upside down except for the flashing neon sign on your back that reads: KICK ME!

When work becomes frustrating—as it always does—most people respond by getting frustrated themselves. The partner who is grumpy in a meeting, for example, gets coworkers who return the favor. (That'll show him.) Who knows whether it's core human nature to mirror behaviors this way or whether we've evolved into it over time, but somewhere along the way the office environment has become a bit more . . . well . . . *tense*.

For example, a Gallup poll showed that one in four employees has a constant feeling of work-related anger. An analysis of the study determined that the primary behaviors that make us want to flip tables are:

1. Being criticized

2. Being ignored

3. Being treated in ways we perceive as "unjust"

Also according to the study analysis, while outright workplace violence does happen, we mostly go rogue without going postal. Rogue behaviors include:

1. Passive-aggressiveness (pretending to comply but being obstructive behind-the-scenes)

2. Procrastinating on purpose

3. Sabotaging projects outright

So, just knowing the top three causes of office frustration (feelings of criticism, neglect, and bias) gives you a starting point in identifying the behaviors you must display to squash them. For example, when handling a difficult situation with a team member, stop and ask yourself three questions:

Am I being kind?

Am I being present?

Am I being fair?

The law of attraction essentially says that you get what you give, so if you want to be on the receiving end of more anger, all you have to do is put anger out in the world. Likewise, if you want an office culture where people genuinely care about each other, you have to start with what you are doing (or not doing) to facilitate that. This sounds simple in theory, of course, but everyone knows that detaching from bad energy is way harder in practice. (Otherwise, those inner critic hobgoblins would be easier to get rid of, right?) Again, the thing to keep in mind—literally—is that the first step is always perception. So. . .

What if you were able to neutralize *every*—yes, every—tense situation at work simply by modeling the behavior you want from colleagues? You can. Here's how.

When The Sh*t Hits the Fan—H.E.A.L.

STEP 1: HIGHLIGHT

The first thing you want to do when confronted by an angry coworker is calmly let the person know she is dangerously close to shifting a logic-based discussion to an emotional one. The trick is to be as gentle as possible because (a) they may be caught up in the moment and completely unaware of their own escalating behavior, and (b) combating aggression with aggression only throws gasoline on the fire. Rest assured, at that point you both will lose. Therefore, all you need to do here is interject a friendly reminder that the other person's tone has gone a bit off the reservation. For instance: *"I'm picking up on some tension here,"* or *"Do you know that you're starting to raise your voice right now?"*

You may even want to chuckle and smile a bit as you are saying this if you think it will help dissolve the tension quicker. But—Holy Disaster—don't try humor unless you're coming from a place of genuine respect. If your attempt to lighten the mood comes off as condescending or sarcastic, this tactic will backfire, big time.

STEP 2: EMPATHIZE

We've all been in frustrating situations at work, and we've all had those times where we wish we wouldn't have gotten as upset as we did. It happens. Give your colleagues the benefit of the doubt that they really don't mean to be rude or heated—they just feel passionate about their ideas. Under normal circumstances, this would be something to embrace. Right now, though, your main job is to *detach from the idea and focus on your response*. If calling attention to the behavior (step 1) hasn't worked, try shouldering some responsibility in your response. For example:

> *Alex, it seems we've had a miscommunication somewhere along the line. I'm sorry if I've made you feel like your idea wasn't being heard or that you were slighted in some way. Please know that wasn't my intention at all. I do think we can come to a solution, but we're going to have to be able to communicate with each other to find it. So, where would you like to go from here?*

There're a couple of powerful things going on here. First, you've implied a certain base level of trust and friendship by using the person's first name, which the human ear tends to register as a verbal pacifier. In other words, it's comforting—especially if you're maintaining a soft tone of voice and looking the other person directly in the eye. Second, by accepting some of the blame for the situation—even if you don't think you deserve it—you're taking a couple of logs off the fire. Again, it's important to reframe your goal here. "Winning" is secondary to your colleague's feelings right now. If your idea gets adopted, but your relationship is irreparably damaged in the process, you haven't won anything at all. Quite the opposite. Third, by putting the ball in the other person's court (i.e., "*Where would you like to go from here?*") you've given that person an opportunity to correct his or her own behavior.

STEP 3: ASK

If your attempts to highlight and empathize aren't working and things have moved rapidly to yelling or something pretty close, now the game changes. As always, your job is to try to defuse the bomb, but this time you have to do it while standing up for yourself simultaneously.

Captain Obvious Alert: Getting to this point should be *extremely* rare in your office or, better yet, shouldn't happen at all. If yelling is common, you are in a toxic dump environment, my friend. Run—don't walk—outta there, fast. Yelling at work is never justified—ever. That said, it does happen, so you need to know how to deal with it so that you don't react in a way that would either humiliate your grandmother or have you running out of the room in tears. This is where your mindfulness comes into play again. If you're thinking, *"I hate this son of a bitch!"* your own behaviors will follow through in step. Your heart will race, your face will turn crimson, and your words will be inarticulate since the part of your brain (cough, cough, prefrontal cortex) that handles executive function is now preoccupied with vengeance. That's obviously a losing strategy. If you're being yelled at, take a moment, breathe deeply, and think about how the only thing you can control is yourself.

A good rule of thumb is to make it your goal to become calmer as the tension levels grow higher. To use an extreme example, if someone is screaming, your response should be at a whisper.

As Stephen Covey famously said in *The Seven Habits of Highly Effective People*, between stimulus and response there is a space, and it's in that space we choose how we wish to respond. Try to get to a point where you can actually observe yourself in communication with others—almost as if you are hovering over your own body and watching your reactions with a box of popcorn. The goal here is to notice your thoughts and intentions *in the moment*, not after the fact. Keep thinking *"I can only control myself"* again and again, take a moment to pause if you need to, and then draw your line in the sand by asking the other person to change their behavior. For example:

I'm truly sorry that you're so upset, but I can't allow anyone to speak to me like this. If you're willing to calm down, I'm happy to stay and discuss a resolution. If not, let's just break here and agree to meet later today or in the morning.

As you're talking, it's important to be acutely aware of your own tone and body language. You want your words to be soft but your stance to be strong. That means:

- No slouching into a defeated, slumped-shoulder posture (stay tall with your spine erect).

- Don't hang your mouth open like you're watching a train wreck (even though you are).

- *Absolutely* no avoidance of eye contact when you're speaking.

Channel your internal Sasha Fierce if you have to, but don't break your calmness *or* your confidence. Period. When the dust settles—and eventually it will—you want to be standing tall.

STEP 4: LEAVE

If all else fails, simply remove yourself from the situation. By now I'm sure you know that I'm not going to recommend storming out. You haven't come this far just to blow it at the end. Rather, all you need to do is grab your things and politely excuse yourself. For example:

> *I can see we're not making any progress so it's probably best to end things here. Alex, I know this has been stressful for you, but it's stressful for everyone else too, and communicating this way doesn't put us any further down the field. Let's take some time to cool off. I'll give you a buzz later this afternoon.*

Assuming the other person is still fuming but no longer yelling, your tone should be like a coach after a losing game— you've had a tough break, but you're still a team for now. You don't need to maintain the strong posture and eye contact that you did in step 3, the "ask" phase, because you don't want to leave with any perceived aggression. This is critically important because the original problem hasn't been addressed with any closure. Therefore, you'll have to meet again to discuss it, so you need the other person out of their karate stance. Three things to keep in mind here.

1. *Do Not Let This Fester.* Seriously, don't wait for Alex to contact you when she calms down. Circle back with her by the end of the day, if possible, or the following morning at the absolute latest. You can't ignore an issue into resolution and— like rotting garbage—the longer it sits the more it will stink!

2. *Do Not Try to Squirm Out of the Situation via E-Mail.* See Chapter 11, "A Note to New Grads," for more on why you should never use e-mail as a medium for resolving a disagreement. (Remember: The message you think you're sending means nothing compared to the one that is received.)

3. *Do Not Trash Your Coworker to Other Colleagues.* Believe me, I understand the temptation to run out of the room and tell someone (anyone!) about how badly you've been wronged. Your mind is most likely whipped into a frenzy replaying what just happened over and over, like a movie in your head—starring you as the victim, of course. *This is precisely the behavior you want to shut down.*

If you've handled the situation using the H.E.A.L. method I've just described (highlight, empathize, ask, and leave), then you've won. The only thing that could derail everything at this point is having your coworker, Alex, hear through the grapevine that you were smack-talking behind her back. In that instant, all of your poise under pressure disappears. Poof! Gone. She won't remember or, better yet, learn from how you handled yourself. She'll only remember you as a back-stabbing, two-faced douchelord.

Crazy only attracts more crazy—and you're not crazy, so don't model behaviors that are.

Finally, and this may sound counterintuitive, problems should be embraced. So rather than think, *"Good God, again? Really?"* think, *"This is a normal part of business."* (It is, after all.) When you view every problem as an inconvenience or a crisis, you're not functioning at a leadership level—not to mention that while your brain is swimming with all that anger, stress, or panic, guess what it's not doing? That's right—*solving the freakin problem!*

Two (Really) Simple Anger Management Techniques

1. *Visualization.* Close your eyes and imagine your anger as water slowly starting to heat within you. Picture it bubbling at your feet and rising up through your legs, torso, arms, and neck. Then, picture the water at a full rolling boil through your head, leaving your body as a plume of steam. Keep your eyes closed and sit with this mental image for a few minutes. Detach from any thoughts about the person or the situation that has infuriated you and focus entirely on the image of the steam and boiling water. Next, picture your body filled with calm water,

swaying gently from left to right, like the liquid within a lava lamp. Keep visualizing this back-and-forth motion in your mind's eye until you feel yourself start to naturally calm down.

2. *Distraction*. Strategically place a favorite photo or a favorite quote as your phone screensaver and in your office. When you're feeling like you're about to blow your stack, focus on it with a *deep* intensity—almost as if you're engaged in a staring contest—until your anger lifts. You want to use the image to take you to your "happy place" and jar you back to internal composure, regardless of what is going on around you. I have a photo of my two boys, ages six and five as I write, in a (rare!) full embrace on my desk. Their genuine affection and toothy, goofy smiles remind me that—regardless of the stress or crisis du jour going on around me—I always have something to be grateful for.

woman 2 woman:
Managing Through Turbulent Times

"I was just a one-year-old when my family emigrated from Kiev to Chicago in search of a better life. What happened next is the epitome of the American dream: With little more than a recipe for a fermented milk drink brought over from Russia, our family built Lifeway Kefir into a multimillion-dollar business that went public in just two years. The driving force behind the company's rapid growth was my father, Michael, who recognized the health benefits of kefir coincided with the exploding natural food market of the late 1980s. But when he died suddenly of a heart attack in 2002, I was thrust into running the business when I was just 27 years old. Now, almost 10 years after that tragic day, Lifeway Kefir is still going strong, growing from $12 million to almost $100 million in sales.

"The sudden and early death of my father was the saddest, most traumatic, and difficult time in my life—and experiencing it publicly made it all the more painful. I suppose I could have lain in bed with the blankets over my head, but instead I repeated, like a mantra, *'Failure is not an option.'* Anything but continued growth and implementation on the strategy we outlined years prior to his death would jeopardize not only the company but what the family had already sacrificed.

"Hindsight is 20/20. I just did what needed to be done every day, no matter what. But I learned fast, failed fast, and tweaked fast. What I lacked in experience I made up for with contagious passion, energy, and innovative thinking. I didn't have time to worry about details or politics. I pride myself in being direct, to the point of being blunt and honest. This forced my team to be empowered and gave both them and myself confidence that together, as a team, we would get to the right place. I have adopted every team member to be like a family member to me, and I am very accepting of all. I think that has fostered a healthy environment; it helps everyone else be honest, if you know you are not being judged, but rather getting feedback or being challenged. Our year-over-year success and growth has created a go-get-'em-can-do atmosphere from the top down. It has helped careers grow and provided an ever-changing evolutionary, positive environment in which [our people] feel they are contributing to the growth of the company.

"Sure, we stumble sometimes . . . but I have learned to stay positive even on the difficult days. As long as we are moving in the right direction, being too focused on the stumbles serves no one. We learn from our mistakes, adapting fast, and I stay optimistic and encourage the team along the way. We are fast and nimble, quick to create trends or spot them early on. Projects are started and completed in days or weeks with very little 'middle management' or long, drawn-out meetings. This keeps our team members motivated, passionate, and inspired and gives them a sense of accomplishment. They are incentivized intrinsically, which frees all of us up to do the work we need to do, rather than just talking about doing the work. I am hands-on, accessible, and involved as requested or required by my team, yet focused on the big picture and long-term opportunities.

"Ten years ago, I could have easily gotten stuck in fear and paralyzed by all that I didn't know. Instead, I played on my strengths with passion, assertiveness, and confidence. Failure has never been, and will never be, an option. There is still much work to be done for Lifeway, for the health of our world, for the plight of girls and women around the world, and even for myself. The ride has been fun, though not easy. I am incredibly grateful to all those who have chosen to go along for it, especially in the early, more unstable days of my leadership."

—Julie Smolyansky, CEO, Lifeway Kefir

·········· **SECTION 4 ROUNDUP** ··········
How to Handle: Tricky Team Situations @ Work

When: A colleague's work is mediocre (at best).

You Should: *Coach through it.* First of all, it's worth noting that no one is perfect. We all have things that pop up and encounter circumstances outside our control that affect our ability to deliver exceptional work all the time.

Traffic is a bitch. Kids get sick. Marriages fail. Computers crash. We get overwhelmed.

In other words, life happens. If an employee's lackluster delivery on a project is unusual or due to one of these or other circumstances that no one can plan for, your best response is to support him as much as possible.

No lecture. No, *"I told you so."* Just you and your team stepping up to fill in the gaps without guilt trips or expected payback. (That's what you'd want him to do for you, right?)

On the other hand, if a recurring pattern of excuses and poor performance becomes apparent, you have to address it. But before you write off the employee as a dud, start with a little internal detective work. First, you want to find out if the person's success metrics were clearly defined—in writing—at the beginning of the project, not midstream. (Sometimes what we think of as "mediocre" is the end result of vague communication.)

Next, you want to dig in to the time allotted for the project. Was it a total rush job? In that case, what did you expect?

But assuming neither of those is the case—congratulations—you're about to demonstrate your capacity for leadership, i.e., that pivotal moment when you can tell someone he's completely disappointing and he still likes you anyway. While most career peeps will tell you to go with the Oreo method of coworker critique—*"You're great"*. . . *"Well, not really"*. . . *"Okay, you're great again"*—I think that's just confusing. Even though two-thirds of your "critique" was positive, your coworker will probably only remember the stinger anyway. So all you have to do is walk over to (or call) your coworker and say something like, *"Hey, Tyson—I'm reading through this video script and I see you have a lot of spelling and segue issues. What's up with that?"*

Now here comes the most important part.

Wait for it . . .

. . . you listen. Give Tyson an opportunity to tell his side of the story. If his reasoning makes sense, ask for ideas on how he'd prevent the situation in the future—but phrase it like you want to brainstorm a few of those ideas on the spot. That way he should feel like you're strategizing with him instead of dropping the hammer on him.

However, if you're not buying the excuses, simply inject a gentle warning: *"Tyson, I appreciate that. Is there anything I can do to help you, because it's my understanding the script was en route to Charlie and, to be honest, I wouldn't want him to see it like this."* Note: The key here is the nonverbals. Tyson needs to understand that his draft is unacceptable but you're still rooting for him to win. Frankly, this is where most managers goof it up.

You don't want Tyson to walk away from the conversation thinking, *"Wow, she really cares about Charlie."* You want him to walk away thinking, *"Wow, she really cares about me."*

Also, keep in mind that a telltale sign of great employees is they actually seek feedback. They want to know how they can improve and tend to take constructive criticism very well. So, if you have someone who never checks in on his work or gets hyper-defensive at every little correction, that's a big red flag you may have someone who isn't a fit with your culture.

For more on this subject, see Chapter 13 and the section on Questions for Underperformance.

When: Your meetings don't feel productive or efficient.

You Should: *Switch it up.* Meetings suck the most when they are either recaps of things that have already happened (yawnfest) or when there are too many damn people in the room (tangent-fest). (If you're heading up a meeting where there are too many people doing recaps, rest assured, everyone wants to kill you.)

Here's another problem: When you have big staff or project meetings with a lot of folks around the table, what you'll quickly discover is that it becomes like a high school cafeteria. There are the "alphas" who dominate (and typically band together) and then there's everyone else.

This is a cultural cancer and a creativity killer.

So get strategic about how you meet with staff. Instead of bringing the whole team in at once, try chatting with one to three people at a time. That way, people will have more breathing room and more opportunity to express their ideas. Also, unless you are giving a presentation where everyone needs to hear the same info all at once, there's no need to have a huge group in the room, anyway.

Another benefit of smaller meetings is that everyone is very clear on their "go-dos." When there are 30 legs under the table, it's easy to pass the buck or to leave the meeting not feeling directly responsible for *anything*. Tiny groups force people to step up, and you can usually knock out who's doing what in half the time.

When: Colleagues keep missing deadlines.

You Should: *Get really good at up-front planning.* Create work plans in advance with clearly defined tasks, owners, and deadlines. Then pad your deadlines by two to three days—but don't tell anyone!—and get the entire team to sign off on the document in advance. This way you'll have some backup later if needed.

That said, before you start browbeating late coworkers with work plans—which will surely put them on the defensive—take a page from the Southern book of charm and pull your offenders aside privately. Look them in the eye and with genuine sincerity, ask: *"Is there any reason why you can't turn in your time sheet on Mondays?"* (This technique works especially well if you have a thick Southern accent but—if you don't—the key is to just be authentic in your tone.) If the other person perceives you as phony or, worse, intimidating, you've completely missed the mark. As discussed in Chapter 13, "The Cure for Fake Harmony," the goal is to use questions to get people talking about their own behavior so they can begin to poke holes in it themselves.

Still, once you've called your team members out on their missed deadlines, you'll need to manage them a little closer moving forward. If they improve, you can back off, but right now they need to know that you're watching. Here are some specific recommendations:

1. *Make sure your coworkers fully "get" what they are supposed to do.* We've all had situations where people come into our office for an assignment, nod in agreement like they understand perfectly, then to go back to their desks frustrated because we "weren't clear." In worst-case scenarios, they'll use confusion on the project as an excuse to sit on it rather than circling back to you with questions. Don't let this slide. Have them repeat the scope of work back to you—including deadlines and delivery format—before turning them loose.

2. *When giving assignments, break them down into smaller chunks on a tighter schedule.* Instead of asking for the full proposal in two weeks, ask for the budget in two days. When the budget is complete, then assign the executive summary that's due in three days—you get the idea. Nine times out of ten, when people miss deadlines it's for one of two reasons. Either they are so overwhelmed by the (perceived) size of a project that they can't seem to get started in the first place, or they put it off until the day of the deadline and then got too slammed with other work to get it all done. The more you know about why your particular teammate is dropping the ball, the more you can manage around it. Also, for larger projects, it's a good idea to actually establish a midpoint check-in—so you could say something like, *"This is due next Thursday, but I'll reach out to you on Tuesday to see how things are going. In the meantime, I'm* *available to answer any questions you have."* This way, you let the other person know you're going to be following up, so it doesn't feel like you're micromanaging and the employee can plan accordingly.

3. *Request Friday Updates.* As discussed previously, I recommend updates that are short, bulleted e-mails listing the week's accomplishments, areas where input is needed, and goals for the week ahead. This way you can keep track of what's getting done and where the holes are.

4. *Don't get loose on your own deadlines.* Think you can hold other people accountable for deadlines when you're missing them yourself? Yeah, lemme know how that goes.

Finally, don't throw your coworkers under the bus with upper management. If you're the leader, guess what? You are accountable for ensuring everyone completes work on time. So if the project was yours and it's late, don't try to weasel out as in, *"We* underestimated how long it would take. . . ." Instead, stand tall and accept the responsibility. Say, *"I* underestimated how long it would take, but now that I know, I'll build in some cushion next time." Assuming you're not in that spot too often, your managers will respect you more for it—and so will your (very relieved) team.

When: You have a team member who monopolizes every discussion.

You Should: *Address it.* Whether people are trying to impress the boss, have a habit of thinking out loud, or just like to hear themselves talk, most teams have players who want all eyes on them. Not only does this suck the energy out of the room, it also just plain *sucks*. It's hard to understand why some people keep talking when everyone else is giving them the SHUT UP! signals. Still, it keeps happening so perhaps those brain scientists are right: *Too much e-communication has reduced our ability to recognize even the most basic facial cues.* If that's you, motor mouth, here are a few universal signals that it's time to pump the brakes:

- Everyone sitting around the table is staring at their crotch.

- You catch colleagues giving each other that unmistakable OMG glance.

- The meeting organizer is looking at you with quasi-bug eyes, hoping you'll wrap up an idea (or take a breath) so that she can interrupt.

Now, if you're not the one hogging the spotlight but work with someone who is, you can test out a few of those nonverbals. (Hey, maybe she's reading.) If that doesn't do the trick, try pulling the person aside after a particularly long-winded episode and say something like, *"I think we made some good progress in there, but it's a shame we didn't get through the entire agenda."* Wait for her response. If she catches on (*"Yeah, I got a little carried away"*) or especially if she doesn't (*"Yeah, we never schedule enough time for these things"*), insert a coaching question: *"Any ideas on how we can hear everyone out while sticking to the time frame?"* Then, gently guide her to the conclusion that individual contributions need to be more focused.

Also, it helps to set the tone up front in your meetings. For example, without singling out anyone in particular, simply make a statement at the beginning that you're going to keep things focused and on track, e.g., *"We don't have a lot of time here and I want to be respectful of all the items we have to cover. Just to keep things moving, may I have your permission to interrupt if we get off topic?"*

Action Plan: Team Development Goals

Select three goals from the following table and write them in the career plan template provided as Tool 1 in the Section 6 Toolbox. (For an e-version of the career plan, please visit www.emilybennington.com/templates.)

Actions	Points
Initiate a company or department-wide volunteer project and coordinate the team. (This is especially effective if you don't manage a team currently but are trying to prove you can.)	15
Volunteer to lead a committee or serve on the board of directors for a nonprofit you care about.	15
Ask your team to provide you with a list of "90-day goals"— that is, a prioritized breakdown of items to be completed within the next three months. (Note: It's important to keep this list short and very high-level.)	15
Successfully navigate through an anger episode using either visualization, distraction, or the H.E.A.L. (highlight, empathize, ask, and leave) method described in detail in Chapter 14.	15

Effectively coach a colleague through a difficult work issue 15
using questions from Chapter 13, "The Cure for Fake
Harmony: 100 Coaching Questions for Team Leaders."

Hire an outside vendor to administer behavioral assess- 15
ments to your team (e.g., DiSC or Myers-Briggs) and
then follow up with training so that employees understand how to function more cohesively as a unit.

At the beginning of your next project, spend a few 10
minutes working with your team to create four to six
behavioral "ground rules." Solicit input from everyone
in the development process and hold team members
accountable (plus, encourage them to hold *each other*
accountable) throughout the process. Here are a few
sample "rules" to get you started.

1. We will support each other.

2. We will set very clear performance expectations and
desired project outcomes.

3. We will proactively seek out all necessary resources
to be successful.

4. We will communicate clearly, frequently, and respon-
sively. (Note: There's nothing that kick-starts office
politics faster than perceived access to communication
and coworkers who try to be "first among equals."
Squash that up front by establishing a set process for
keeping everyone in the loop.)

Meet with your team individually at the beginning of 10
the project for a "get to know you" chat. (See Chapter
13 for a list of "Getting to Know You Questions.")

When sending reports to upper management, include   5
the name(s) of contributing team members on the
title page.

Applaud your team members' efforts—literally. If a   5
coworker has done something worthwhile, have the
entire team give that person a standing ovation at the
next meeting. This will make her feel great—and there's
no charge.

p a r t   t h r e e
align with what works

You ready to walk the walk?

Section 5:
LEADERSHIP

1	2	3	4	5
Self-Awareness	Social Skills	Personal Effectiveness	Team Development	Leadership
				↑ You are here.

Core Principle

You inspire others to freely give the best of themselves by being a model of kindness, integrity, commitment, and results. You take a big-picture, long-lens approach to all situations and gently guide others to do the same.

In this section, you will learn how to:

- Think of yourself as a leader.

- Build influence (even without authority).

- Turn your colleagues into champions.

What Your Coworkers Are Thinking

"Amanda is someone I want to follow."

CHAPTER FIFTEEN

having authority is like having a gun in your closet

there if you need it, but hopefully you won't have to pull the trigger

WHAT DO YOU *feel is most lacking in your workplace?*

It was a key question in a survey I gave to the women's network of a Fortune 500 company.

At the top of their list?

Leadership.

However, when the same 60 executive women were asked to rank their own leadership ability on a scale of 1 to 5 (1 = poor and 5 = outstanding), no one ranked themselves a 5.

Not one.

It doesn't take a genius to figure out why leadership may be missing from the organization as a whole—*if it's not in the people, it's not going to be in the business*. Still, when I traveled to the corporate headquarters to deliver the survey results in person, I didn't find a room full of wallflowers. On the contrary, these women were extremely poised and self-assured. So what happened?

Upon further inspection, the hesitation for these women executives to call themselves "leaders" didn't stem from an *under*-inflated confidence level, but from an *overly* inflated perception of the word.

I'm generalizing here but basically *"leader"* felt like a word other people should use to describe them, and not a way to describe themselves.

Well, isn't that humble . . . not to mention *completely insane*! Seriously, can you imagine those findings in a group of F500 men? Of course not. And the impact on your career is huge because if you don't see yourself as a leader, no one else will either.

So . . . let's all take a deep breath and get comfortable with this word, shall we? Say it with me now: L-E-A-D-E-R. That's right. L-E-E-E-E-E-E-E-E-E-E-E-E-E-A-D-E-R. Look, I know it's easy to identify "leadership" with a specific job title and to feel like you won't "be" a leader until you've hit that milestone. But leadership isn't about a rung on the ladder; it's about *influence*—and there are people all around you demonstrating leadership skills (or not) every day simply by living their lives in a way that inspires others to want to be better (or not).

That's the secret formula—it's not pushing, it's *pulling*. When people ask me about the difference between team development and leadership, I always say team development is about getting the best from your people, but leadership is about inspiring them to get the best *from themselves*. You can't do that by hitting them over the head with a stick (authority); you do it by holding out a carrot (influence) and saying, *"Come get it."* If you aspire to leadership roles, mastering this process is the very fabric of your success.

Leading from Where You Are

Okay . . . so the first thing you should know about influence (with or without authority) is that it's simply a matter of *leading from where you are*. It's about motivating people and getting the best performance from teams regardless of what your business card says or whether you're operating from a peer level or a supervisor level. Tough one, huh? That's because this is a real chicken-and-egg deal. When you become the boss you get authority, but you can't use authority to become the boss. (I'm not knocking authority, mind you. I'm just saying you can't use it as your only tool in the shed to get things done.)

Think about it: Maybe you've worked for bosses in the past who pulled rank or liked to throw their weight around. If so, my guess is you probably *despised* those jobs. It's a pretty useless tactic that doesn't get anyone very excited about their work. So authority on its face is a very poor determination of what makes a leader. On the other hand, *influence* is. Because when you lead by influence, you are inspiring, serving, and nurturing others— which means your whole approach is to make the people around you feel excited about the purpose of *their* work and *their* opportunity to contribute. These are obviously two very different ways to lead and typically they have two very different outcomes.

If you want to be a leader, the word you should be focused on every day is "trust." When coworkers *trust* you, they'll not only do more for you, but your ideas will get adopted faster, coworkers will bring more excitement and enthusiasm to their work with you, you'll get more information and support from your teams, and—eventually—you'll get pulled off the bench for bigger opportunities down the road. (Also, for those of you who are directly serving clients, you already know that when customers trust you, they buy more, they lean on you more, and they recommend you more.) This is all good stuff, right?

So to understand where you are in the context of leadership, the question you need to ask yourself is, *"Can teammates trust me?"*

First and foremost, trust is built on *dependability*. (Those of you who have read *Effective Immediately* know I love me some words ending in "-ility.") In other words, do you do what you say you are going to do when you say you're going to do it? This is the linchpin of everything else because, if your coworkers can't rely on you, you have no trust—which means you have no influence.

I spoke with a young woman who graduated college less than a year ago who is working for a Fortune 50 company and already in charge of a project where she has multiple people reporting to her across different departments in her company— most of whom have been with the organization a very long time. Think authority would work here? Me either. This woman is excelling in her position, though, because she knows how important it is for every member of her team to see—with their own eyes—that she's not only capable of being high-level and strategic, but she's also in the trenches with them and isn't afraid to do the work and get her hands dirty too. *That's* dependability. Understanding where you are in the leadership picture means you have to pay attention to your own behaviors not only because you want to rock out in your current role—which you do—but also because you want to prove yourself as worthy to move on to bigger and better things.

Meeting Other People Where They Are

Of course, building influence means meeting other people where they are as well. For example, since you picked up a book with "domination" in the title, perhaps you're the type who tends to make decisions pretty quickly and intuitively. Like, it's painful for you to sit and listen to other people finish their thoughts because you've already worked out the solution in your head and you're ready to blurt out the next steps as you see them.

But . . . let's say you are on a project team and one of the key contributors is Dom, who's introverted and emotional. He's older than you and has a great reputation, so you want to be respectful, but you're also getting a bit frustrated with Dom's long-winded responses to basic questions and what you perceive as an overly analytical nature. This is a challenge, right? How are you supposed to co-create with someone when you obviously have two entirely different work styles? I mean, do you call him out on it? Or do you just go with the flow? The mistake that many rookie leaders will make is to think they can change Dom into becoming more direct. You may want Dom to be like you, but the truth is—Dom can only be like Dom. You can't mold or morph him into becoming more of what you want unless it's something that he wants, too. Therefore, the only option you have is to meet Dom where he is.

This requires some patience, obviously, as well as some adapting and finesse on your part—but it also requires something else.

What if I told you that "team synergy" was something *you can control* rather than a matter of chance or some arbitrary stroke of luck? For example, most of us go through life believing that the notion of liking someone (or not liking someone) is completely random. Have you ever had any of the following thoughts:

"I wonder if they'll like me."

"I wonder if I'll like them."

"What if I hate my new client?"

Sounds familiar, doesn't it? That's because it's how the majority of us have been conditioned to think. Take the last example: *"What if I hate my new client?"* That line of thinking sort of leaves things to chance, doesn't it? Here's a new way to look at it: What if you *decided* to like your client? This is the concept of selective liking. And by that I mean there is no question. You simply make it so. You leave it to your mind and your will to assign the liking rather than crossing your fingers and hoping it all works out. Seriously, how much sense does this makes in terms of all of your work relationships? Selective liking is a game-changer, and when you understand this paradigm and apply it to your life, you have a big advantage.

Of course, it's worth noting here that you *need* diverse people to produce superior results, so it will also help if you approach differences in general as a very healthy part of what it means to be a team. How do you think any solution originated by a group of people who acted and thought just like you would turn out? Likely pretty limited, eh? It wouldn't have much depth, or richness or creativity. Now, contrast that to what a group of divergent thinkers would come up with. Envision a team that has a mix of quick-thinkers, slow-thinkers, intuitives, introverts, extroverts, younger, older, male, female, from many backgrounds and geographies . . . The point here is that we all *need* the "Doms" and others on our teams, especially if we want to produce a worthy end product.

So let's jump back to dealing with Dom. If your work styles are different, how can you jive together? When you employ selective liking, you simply don't view your differences as a negative. Rather than feeling "stuck," you look for things you can like about Dom rather than spinning your wheels on all the things you don't. And when you choose to like someone, it affects how you treat that person across the entire spectrum of your work together, including how you communicate, how you listen, how patient you are, and how willing you are to go out of your way to help him— all of which, of course, affects how willing he is to help you.

No Like-y? No Problem

Again, the first step to meeting others where they are is choosing to like and accept them *as they are*. Naturally, you will have to adapt your communication style to get things done, right? Yep . . . of course you will, but this is what separates girls from women.

Again, think of the bosses who lead with authority first. Usually what you'll find is that they have one communication style—their own. But one size never fits all, and if you want to have influence, you have to not only have the ability to recognize different personality types, you also have to respond differently to each. I know this advice may seem complex; but let me give you an example. Let's return to you as the extroverted, direct communicator and Dom as the introverted, long-winded harmonizer on your team. Knowing that you can't force Dom to adopt your direct style and that you've already chosen to appreciate Dom for who he is (which, by the way, is someone very good at his job)—what do you do?

Well, we already know that you (desperately) want to interrupt Dom as he's speaking—but let's think for a minute about how that could make him feel. Remember the saying, *"People may forget what you say or do, but they never forget how you made them feel?"* That concept is never tested more than when two people have fundamentally different communication styles.

In this case, listening more could be an area where you must learn to adapt. Maybe you've come to expect that Dom will not always initiate with you first. Instead of just assuming that if you haven't heard from him he must not have anything to say, what if you reached out to him occasionally to ask his opinion? We know Dom is long-winded, so it will take a few extra minutes of your time, but it will also help him feel respected and so it's probably a good investment. Same goes for meetings or group settings—Dom may not be comfortable jumping into a fast-paced discussion, so you can make a point to ask for his input. Now, if you go out of your way to do these things, do you think you'll have earned Dom's respect? Of course. And as a by-product you'll have earned additional influence.

Influence *Right Now*

What else can you do—immediately—to be a leader with or without the title? Let's dive into this idea a little further. I want you to think about someone from your life—someone you know personally—who you consider a world-class leader. Maybe you're thinking of a coach, a boss, a professor . . . or even a parent in business. Now, I assume all of those folks have authority, but I'll bet you that if you studied their backgrounds, what you'd find is that they became very adept at leadership—at motivating, influencing, and empowering others—before they earned their title. That's because all great leaders excel at getting a team to rally around them—but what they are actually doing, underneath it all, is getting the team to rally around itself and all team members to rally around themselves.

I'll bet the person who came to your mind as a great leader is actually someone who makes *you* feel like you're competent and capable of doing anything. Maybe this person pulled you outside your comfort zone—but it was because she believed in you and wanted to see you stretch yourself. That's the feeling great leaders pass on. But—believe me—you don't need a fancy title to do it. If you are someone who inspires others to *connect with their own power*, I promise you that, over time, you *will* garner influence at work because others will view you as someone who is going to help *them* win. Your coworkers will sense that you are on the fast track and they will want to support you because they know it will inevitably benefit them, too.

A Case Study in Influence Without Authority: The (True) Story of the San Francisco Penguins

A few years ago, the San Francisco Zoo had a problem: Forty-six penguins who had been long-time residents simply stopped swimming. The zookeepers were completely scratching their heads to figure out why these penguins, who evidently used to be quite active, were now only taking occasional dips in the pool to cool off and . . . well, basically . . . that was it. Imagine, 46 sunning penguins just lying around, getting fat, living a pretty easy, complacent life. Not only was it unhealthy for the penguins to live this way, but it also couldn't have been much fun for the visitors, either.

So the zoo brought in six new penguins. These were transfers from another zoo and, when they moved in, they starting doing what normal penguins do. Which is to say they immediately jumped into the pool and swam . . . and swam . . . and swam. And to the amusement of the staff and visitors—and the total curiosity of the 46 other penguins—the six newcomers swam laps all day long. Day after day. They didn't fight or squawk with the penguins who were already there, and they didn't try to persuade them to join in. They just went about their business of swimming in circle after circle around the pool.

And then something pretty cool happened.

One by one, all of the original 46 penguins started to join in. They changed their lazy habits and began swimming all day as well. What's amazing about this story—aside from the fact that it's true—is that just six penguins had influence over the other 46 without arguing or cajoling—only by *doing*. They were "being the change" and, lo and behold, that made all the difference.

woman 2 woman: *Finding Your Voice*
"I'll never forget my first day at *Vogue*. My office was in a closet, basically, I didn't know many people, and I had just moved back to New York City from Paris, so I was experiencing a bit of a cultural shock. Everyone who worked there seemed larger than life, people like Carlyne Cerf de

Dudzeele, André Leon Talley, and Grace Coddington. They were very much the creative lifeblood of *Vogue* back in those days. It was a visual magazine—still is in many ways—but then the writers and features editors played second fiddle to the stylists. I wasn't really sure where, as a writer, I would fit in, but I figured out pretty quickly that the people who created the visuals needed someone to articulate their ideas and to balance the magazine by making the stories told in text as strong and well crafted as those told in pictures.

"I am a reporter. I love stories—writing them, hearing them, telling them, and so that quickly became my niche at *Vogue*. I became the information gatherer. I reported on shows, I hung out backstage, I listened to the designers talk about the inspiration for their collections, and I translated everything into stories for the magazine—runway reports, designer profiles, trend pages, you name it. I kept my ear to the ground, I answered my own phone—most of the time—I listened to every pitch, and I worked incredibly hard. I certainly didn't come into my position with any authority, but before long, I not only earned the respect of my colleagues, I found my place and my voice at the magazine—even among a field of incredible fashion icons. That experience taught me that once you find your voice you can do anything."

—Kate Betts, contributing editor of
Time magazine (former fashion director at
Vogue and editor-in-chief of *Harper's Bazaar*)

CHAPTER SIXTEEN

that's great and all, but nobody knows who you are

DARNELL IS A very talented attorney in a corporate law firm. She had worked her way up from entry-level paralegal to just under partner status in 15 years . . . and by "worked," I mean this girl *worked*. When everyone else was going home for the evening, Darnell's green light (signaling she was logged in to her network computer) was still on. When you sent her an e-mail, regardless of whether it was 11:00 a.m. or 11:00 p.m., you got an answer almost immediately.

Darnell was respected by colleagues in her office and held a leadership position as co-administrator of the firm-wide customer relationship management (CRM) process. But she felt ready to do more. Much more. She was hoping the company's annual two-day CRM planning meeting would be a chance to showcase her skills and, since the C-level team would be in attendance, Darnell had spent weeks ensuring that every detail was in place—from making sure there were branded napkins for the opening reception to personally formatting the presentation graphics. Fortunately, she had Bob—her partner in the CRM process—to help. Bob and Darnell worked well together and he was instrumental in helping her plan the event and making sure everything ran smoothly.

But here's where Bob outsmarted her.

On the morning after the opening reception—while Darnell was in the conference room ensuring that the A/V was working and swag bags were arranged—Bob was at the hotel having breakfast with the firm's executive team. It wasn't an intentional shut-out. Darnell had been invited, too, but she felt so over-whelmed with the logistics of the meeting that she politely declined. Despite her absence, Bob, who was two decades older than Darnell and viewed her as somewhat of a protégé, graciously praised her work at the breakfast in front of, essentially, her boss's boss's boss. When he later mentioned it to Darnell, she turned into a schoolgirl asking about her first crush.

You talked about me? Really? Well, what did he say? Did he enjoy the reception? Is he pleased? Seriously, what did he say?

Bob had to deliver the news that the boss's boss's boss didn't say much of anything. When Bob mentioned what a great job Darnell had done on the event, the CEO was happy of course, but—well—that was it. The subject quickly changed and that was that. No lingering discussion on what a valuable addition to the team she was. No kudos for all of the work she had put into the event so far. Just a quick, *"That's wonderful!"* and on to the next conversation topic.

Obviously, this was disappointing news. Sure, there were 1,500 people in the firm, but Darnell genuinely thought the CEO would know enough about her individual contributions to be able to talk about them freely. Instantly, her mind started spinning with all of the things she wished he would have said when her name was mentioned, things like, *"Oh yeah! I know Darnell. She's a real superstar, that one,"* or *"Yes, I wish she had been able to join us here. I'd love to catch up with her."*

Now, Darnell's big mistake was assuming that if she met her billable-hour quota and kept her head down, the firm's leadership—some 300 miles away, mind you—would know how talented she was. What she failed to realize, however, was that this wasn't a solid career strategy. So while there's no doubt she was working hard, the fact that the executive team didn't understand her value meant Darnell wasn't exactly working smart.

What's Your Worth?

If you want an easy way to determine whether you are valued at work, try this: Pitch a (good) idea to your supervisors that would logically increase sales or productivity. Then wait and see what happens.

Immediate action = Congratulations!

No response = Not good.

Of course, this isn't a foolproof experiment; you may work for a responsive company or your managers could take forever to get back to you but green-light the idea anyway. The point is that the way in which your team responds will be oh-so-telling. Why?

Because when you're valued, *people jump*.

Not to mention, when you're valued, people don't just listen —they *galvanize*. Naturally, all of this is directly proportional to the perceived contribution you are bringing to the table. The more your coworkers can tie you and your work to the company's success, the more respect you will get. Therefore, if you don't feel valued at work, the root cause is probably one of three things:

1. You're not doing a good job.

2. Your office culture stinks.

3. Your colleagues don't understand what you do.

Assuming you're pulling your weight and the culture is fine, let's focus on the latter issue. If you're like Darnell and many other women, you are probably very bad at making your achievements known. There's something in our double-X chromosome that likes to assume if we're doing a good job, our colleagues already know. Problem is, they often *don't* know—typically because they're too busy worrying about their own achievements. So this is where you have to step up and raise your profile by bragging . . . *a lot*.

Easy there, partner. I didn't say you had to brag on yourself. (That's a one-way ticket to Camp Asshole.) The trick is that you have to be so good that others can't help but brag about you. Because here's a little corporate reality:

The vast majority of decisions affecting your career trajectory will happen behind closed doors when you're not in the room.

In other words, when the next big project comes up, or the company is evaluating who to send to the conference, or who is the best candidate for the promotion, there's a good chance it won't be your supervisor making those calls alone. It will usually be a team of executives sitting around a conference table weighing the pros and cons of who gets the job. Now the question becomes, *"What's going to happen when your name pops up?"* As in Darnell's case, if the people who work directly with you think you're swell but no one else knows you exist—that's a huge problem. So you need to actively turn colleagues into advocates who will champion you when it counts . . . over and over again.

The Difference Between Mentors and Sponsors

It's been said that women in business today are overmentored and undersponsored. If you're thinking *"What's the diff?"* keep in mind that mentors are concerned with your professional development, while sponsors are concerned with your professional *achievements*.

For example, a mentor may say, *"Let me know if you have any questions,"* but a sponsor would say, *"Let me call the division leader and see if there are any openings."* Big distinction.

Your job is to seek out as many sponsors for your career as possible. This is where the coaching leadership model is critical, because when colleagues respect and trust you, they'll be more willing to stand up for you behind those closed doors.

That said, you can't work with everyone in your company directly, so you also have to take the reins and actively seek to raise your own profile where it counts. That means being strategic about the people you should know (and should know you) and finding ways to get on their radar. Many techniques have been discussed in this book so far. Perhaps—like Valarie Gelb (see Chapter 1)—you cleverly get yourself invited to key meetings. Or perhaps—like my friend at Microsoft (see Chapter 10)—you create your own Career Development Plan and share it with senior leaders. Whatever your tactic, don't sit back and "hope" you'll get noticed on work alone because, like Darnell, you'll get lost in the crowd.

woman 2 woman: On Networking

"If I could go back to the very beginning of my career and do one thing differently, it would be to understand the value of networking. I have always been a believer that outstanding performance and results are the drivers of a successful career. I thought that if I worked hard enough, I'd produce results, be noticed and automatically be considered for key projects or promotional opportunities, and achieve my professional and personal goals. I am still a believer that there is no substitute for hard work and strong performance, but what I learned over time is that being successful is about more than just doing your job well—it is also highly influenced through the learning that takes place and the exposure gained by building a strong internal and external network of contacts. In my case, I work in a very large company with operations in more than 80 countries. I was highly successful in operational leadership in my geographic area, but I did not have exposure to the many opportunities that arose nationally or internationally. And as I did not have a strong network outside of my own division and geography, even though I was a strong performer, when opportunities arose, I was not always on the radar screen.

"I was fortunate that when I was ready for my next professional move, my company was launching a series of employee network groups. I volunteered to cochair the regional chapter for our women's network group and immediately connected with a wide range of professionals from the many different business lines, and eventually [that experience] gave me national exposure as a leader. In this role, I was able to truly appreciate the benefits of networking—I learned so much about my company, including the many different business lines, and I also was exposed to so many different perspectives from the professionals within the network group.

"This experience led me to the realization that it was important for me to enhance my own professional development and to position myself for future promotional opportunities—to make sure that I built in the time to lift my head up from work and take a look around, and connect with professionals inside our company and external in our industry. I soon joined the Women's Foodservice Forum, an external professional association devoted to elevating women leaders, and volunteered to chair various committees. Again, it was a fabulous opportunity for me to expand my network, grow professionally, and bring back new knowledge and perspectives to my company. Later, I became involved with several industry advisory boards as well as the governance board of the Multicultural Foodservice and Hospitality Alliance.

"Eventually, I moved into a national role within Sodexo as the VP for sourcing and talent acquisition. Although I know that I obtained this role because of my professional skill and knowledge, I also believe that the contacts, perspectives, and exposure I had gained through networking helped. Over time, I have found that my network continues to provide value by expanding my horizon and access to a whole range of professionals. I have also learned the importance of giving back to my network—sharing my own knowledge and expertise with others to promote mutual learning and success."

—Arie Ball, vice president, sourcing
and talent acquisition, Sodexo, Inc.

"Getting to know people within your industry is something that I make sure I tell everyone. Going outside of the work environment, attending meet and greets, and dropping a card wasn't exactly a top priority for me at the beginning of my career. In hindsight, networking would have helped me then, but it's certainly more important than ever now."

—Ingrid Ciprian-Matthews,
vice president, CBS News

How to Handle: Tricky Leadership Situations @ Work
••

When: You have a staffer who thinks he should be leading the team.

You Should: *Stand your ground.* As you move into leadership roles within your organization, you'll no doubt bump into situations where a colleague either wants a leadership position you hold—or perhaps even wants your job itself. While it's tempting to show your teeth and snarl like a dog backed into a corner, you still have to work with this person, so you have to keep him engaged *and* keep the peace. It may be extremely difficult, since there's a good chance your coworker will try to prove himself capable of the job by making you look incapable—especially when there's an audience around. Whatever you do, don't lose your cool! Instead, pull him aside afterward and say something like this:

"Mike, I know you've been here for a while and have strong feelings about how projects should be managed, but when you routinely question my decisions on these calls, it creates negative energy for the whole team. You've got some great ideas and I want you to feel free to express them, but once a decision has been made to move forward, I need you on my side. Otherwise, that negative energy is going to start affecting the whole group and we can't let that happen. If something isn't working right or is bothering you, please come talk to me about it privately. My door is always open. I promise we will address it immediately and bring everyone else up to speed if needed. Otherwise, let's agree that once final plans are in motion we'll keep the calls positive, so everyone can feel good about the work we're doing here."

If that doesn't work, you'll have to get Mike's boss involved. Ideally, you'll want her to schedule a private meeting with Mike to clarify what his role is (and isn't) and what your role is. (Note: It will probably be more impactful to Mike if you're not in this meeting. Otherwise, he'll assume you're behind it.)

Also, you know the saying, *"Keep your friends close and your enemies closer?"* While I don't want to encourage you to think of coworkers as enemies, the general idea certainly applies here. So if all else fails, put aside your anger for a moment and invite Mike to coffee. That's right. Ask about his plans and future goals within the company—and even whether there's anything you can do to support him along the way. You might discover that Mike only *thinks* he wants your position because it's what he sees right in front of him, while in fact there are multiple opportunities for him to get involved in different areas where you won't step on each other's toes.

When: You have an employee who wants a promotion, but you're not sure she's ready.

You Should: *Make 'em "Prove They're Worth It."* I'm embarrassed to admit it, but I asked Skip for a promotion after just nine months in the workforce. Fortunately for both of us, he had a super-savvy way to handle it. First, he listened. He didn't try to convince me that I was too inexperienced or that nine months on the job was a little early to start gunning to move up. Instead, he heard me out and, after I made my case, he said he'd give it some thought. Then, a few days later he presented me with a simple one pager called "Prove You're Worth It." It was a list of 10 tasks, and I had to pick seven of them to complete—

in addition to keeping up with the responsibilities of my current role. The list included tasks such as picking a system in the office I felt could be improved and writing a plan for how to fix it, hosting a Lunch 'n Learn for the staff, creating a SWOT (Strengths, Weaknesses, Opportunities, Threats) analysis on myself, and reading a classic business book and writing a summary of what I learned and how I was going to apply it to my job. Next, he asked me to check in with him every time I completed a task or if I had any questions along the way. After that, I was on my own. It took me about six months to get all seven tasks completed, but when everything was said and done . . . I got the promotion—and Skip got to buy some time. But more than that, he also got to evaluate how I handled stress, how I solved problems, how committed I was, and what kind of attitude I would bring to jumping through those hoops to earn my new position. This was definitely a win-win for both of us and an exceptional management strategy.

When: You can dish out constructive criticism but you can't take it.

You Should: *Get over yourself.* Sure, you've proven that you are skilled on the job—and that's what has brought you to this point in your career. But self-perception will get you only so far. To go even further, you need to dig into external perceptions. (If we all lived inside our minds, then it wouldn't matter, but we don't, so it does.) In that sense criticism is a gift that's incredibly ripe with valuable information. Hard to take sometimes, but worth selectively and appropriately pursuing, nonetheless. For example, let's say a colleague tells you she'd like to see a little more creativity in your work, or that your deadlines for review and approvals are too tight. Whatever it is, accept it—actually, make that embrace it—at full face value. Then, study and reflect upon it. After you've thanked your colleague for sharing her feedback with you, go away and ponder what you heard. If others have this perception about you, what could be the contributing factors? This is a great opportunity to consult with a trusted colleague or your supervisor, to get another perspective if needed. Then, when you've reflected on it a bit, *act*. Distill it all down to a list of a few critical items. In other words, what do you need to do to improve your creativity, writing skills, timing on deadlines, or whatever? It doesn't have to be a lengthy exercise, but it will certainly be an invaluable one if taken seriously.

When: You're running a volunteer project for a nonprofit, but you're frustrated because none of your committee members are doing anything.

You Should: *Practice back-to-the-basics management.* First, schedule your meeting at lunchtime and either make the nonprofit pay for it or collect a lunch fund from members. (Note: You want to serve a nice lunch, not a tray of cold cuts on white bread with American cheese. Yes, I know it's a nonprofit, but proper brainpower needs proper fuel. Plus, you want to send a message that you respect your members and value their time.)

Second, have a clear agenda that you send to participants two to three days in advance: Any longer and they won't look at it, and any shorter is rude. Make sure everything (I mean everything) on your agenda has a *decision* and/or *action steps* attached to it, and that the caliber of the work fits the caliber of the room. I once attended a meeting where our team of rock-star executives went line-by-line through a press kit at the request of the committee chair. Imagine an hour of questions like, *"Do you think we should add a comma here?"* or *"Is there a way to join these two sentences?"* (Seriously, waterboarding would have been less torturous.)

Third, it's a common problem to have committee members who are great at tossing out ideas but duck into their turtle shells when it comes to implementation. (Shocking, I know.) This doesn't make them bad people; it just means you have to get tougher as the leader. For example, if one of your members says, *"I think we should send out a mailing,"* grab your pen and say, *"I agree. Would you like to be in charge?"* This response does two things: First, you'll notice the number of grand ideas thrown into the pool shrinks—which is actually good because, presumably, the ones people are brave enough to mention will be vetted. Second, it gets the team engaged. As the leader, you obviously shouldn't be doing less work than your committee, but you shouldn't leave with your name beside all the tasks, either. If members aren't stepping up on what needs to get done, simply start assigning (e.g., decide who is best suited for a task, look her directly in the eye, and say, *"Ann, would you be willing to contact Dave to see if the room is available on the 14th?"*). Then, by the end of the day, send a short, bulleted e-mail recap of decisions made, tasks assigned, responsible parties, and the next meeting date.

Fourth, every meeting you chair, whether it's for your company or for a nonprofit, should have a hard start and stop time. If you're running a group of volunteers, keep it to an hour max—otherwise it'll be tough to get people to show up, regardless of how good lunch is.

One final note: If you have team members who are just not contributing despite your best efforts, it's important to avoid any outward signs of frustration—they are volunteering their time, after all. Instead, give them an honorable way out. You could say, *"Deb, I appreciate your being part of this committee, but I know you've got a lot on your plate at work right now."* Wait for the response, which hopefully will be along the lines of, *"You're right,"* opening the door for a coaching question: *"Do you think a hiatus from the committee would help?"*

Action Plan: Leadership Goals

Select three goals from the following table and write them in the career plan template provided as Tool 1 in the Section 6 Toolbox. (For an e-version of the career plan, please visit www.emilybennington.com/templates.)

Action	Points
Send Friday Updates to your boss, team, and/or clients clients each week for a month, outlining your accomplishments, areas where input is needed, and goals for the week ahead. Remember: Friday Updates are bulleted lists and shouldn't take you more than 10 to 15 minutes each to create. (Once you start sending Friday Updates, there's a good chance your team/clients will find them so helpful they'll start to expect them. Consider yourself warned.)	15
Take the Leadership Readiness Assessment in the Toolbox in Section 6 (15 bonus points if you ask a colleague to assess you as well).	15

Participate in an internal (ideally) or external leadership development program.	15
Create a list of key influencers (a.k.a. potential sponsors) within your organization. Find legitimate reasons to get on their radar.	15
Reach out to someone you respect in your company. Tell this person why she inspires you and invite her to meet for coffee or tea.	15
Invite a younger or less experienced colleague to lunch. Talk about her aspirations and future career plans. Share what you've learned about virtues-centered living.	15
Be a mentee in your company's formal program.	15
Serve as a mentor in your company's program.	15
Purchase a business book for your team members and host a meeting to discuss important lessons from the text and how they relate to your project/company.	15
Study people who own their power. How do they show confidence without arrogance? How are they pleasing, but not overly eager to please? Note your observations in a career journal.	10
Create your own personal affirmation related to leadership. It could be a favorite quote or a spin-off of your virtues list. Keep it in a place where you can refer to it often.	10
Post on your company's internal blog (if you have one).	5

Nominate a deserving colleague for a "40 Under 40" award or other industry honor.	5
Send a coworker an e-mail, with a manager cc'd, applauding the person for a job well done.	5

toolbox

Tool 1: Career Plan Template

Select three goals that you commit to achieving from the Action Plan tables at the end of Sections 1–5. Write each goal in the career plan template below . . . then get started. At the end of your 60-day deadline, tally up the points of your completed tasks and assess your rock star potential on the following Promotability Scale. (For an e-version of the career plan, please visit www.emilybennington.com/templates.)

Today's Date: _____

60-Day Deadline: _____

Exercises	Points	Deadline	Date Completed
Self-Awareness			
1.			
2.			
3.			
Social Skills			
1.			
2.			
3.			
Personal Effectiveness			
1.			
2.			
3.			
Team Development			
1.			
2.			
3.			

Exercises	Points	Deadline	Date Completed
Leadership			
1.			
2.			
3.			

Total Points Earned: _____

Promotability Scale

Total Points	Promotability
225 and above	Rock Star (*Yeah!*)
150–224	Backup Band (*Meh*)
75–149	Groupie (*Ewww*)
74 and under	Nosebleed Seats (*Sigh . . .*)

Tool 2: Six-Month Check-In Template

One of the things I always enjoyed about corporate recruiting was the insight into what my company viewed as the "ideal employee." When meeting candidates at career fairs or in our office, we would usually have them speak with two or three firm partners and staffers, who would then rate each candidate on a score sheet similar to the template below. (Yes, it's a cold process, but it's efficient.) Afterward, all the interviewers would huddle in a conference room and pick our favorites. (Some of your most important career decisions happen when you're not in the room, remember?)

I saw a lot of eager candidates turn into full-time hires and then, over the years, I watched as they moved up, left, or stayed in the same spot while others advanced around them. Notably, the ones who didn't cut it usually gave a great interview—jumped onboard with gusto—then fizzled out, while the ones lapping everybody else were consistently solid in the same areas that got them hired in the first place.

So what are those areas for *your* company? Do you even know? If not, hit up your colleagues in HR or recruiting and request a copy of your organization's interview evaluation form. When you have it in hand, ask yourself the all-important question: *If I were to be interviewed again, right now, would I be hired against a field of other qualified candidates?*

Don't round the corners on any qualities your company takes seriously enough to screen for at the entry level.

If you can't get a copy of your company's interview evaluation form, here's a general version you can use. Rank yourself in these areas at least once every six months, channeling that sharp-edged, *something-to-prove attitude* you had when you were first hired, and bringing that unbridled energy to work with you now.

Qualifications	Awesomeness	Average	Not Even Close
Grooming (professional appearance, appropriate attire, tidy workspace)			
Preparation (meeting deadlines, asking smart questions, read/organized materials in advance of meetings)			
Enthusiasm (self-starter, easy to talk to, sense of humor, positive spirit of someone who is happy to be here)			
Executive Presence (composed, skillfully able to diffuse tough conversations)			
Commitment (willingness to work hard, disciplined, focused, results-oriented)			
Communication Skills (clear and concise, thoughtful, assertive when needed, direct without being offensive)			

Tool 3: Personal Career Assessment

Today's Date: _____

Part 1: Here's another tool you can use as a quick career "pulse check." To begin, rate yourself on a scale of 1 to 5 in each area, noting that 1 = outstanding and 5 = poor.

■   ■   ■

Self-Awareness: You take full responsibility for your own mind, body, and career with a daily practice focused on the process of continued growth and improvement.

1	2	3	4	5

_____

_____

_____

Social Skills: You enjoy harmonious relationships at work because you are a force of positive energy who can be counted on to "show up," communicate with respect, and (when needed) disagree without being abrasive.

1	2	3	4	5

_____

_____

_____

Personal Effectiveness: You have a clear understanding of your personal core values and a way to measure progress on how well you achieve them. In your job, you not only deliver what's asked of you on time and on budget, but you regularly bring new ideas to the table as well. You have a solid grasp of your individual success metrics and consistently engage in training and development to stay razor-sharp in all aspects of your performance.

1   2   3   4   5

_____

_____

_____

_____

Team Development: You have the ability to draw the best performance from others because you create an environment where all team members have a clear understanding of their responsibilities, the resources needed to be successful, and feel safe to express their opinions.

1   2   3   4   5

_____

_____

_____

_____

Leadership: You inspire others to freely give the best of themselves by being a model of kindness, integrity, commitment, and results. You take a big-picture, long-lens approach to all situations and gently guide others to do the same.

1   2   3   4   5

_____

_____

_____

_____

Assuming you didn't rate yourself a 1 in each area (*and if you did, why did you buy this book, eh?*), now you know where you need to focus the most time and energy in your professional development.

. . .

Part 2: Now let's take this assessment a step further and noodle on two questions for a moment.

1. What kept you from earning a score of 1?

2. What would a perfect score in each area actually look like?

In the lined spaces provided below each category, spend a few minutes jotting down the specific reason(s) for your score and what actions would take you to a 1.

Also, if you're really brave, give this assessment to your colleagues. Ask them to rate you and compare their results to yours.

Tool 4: Leadership Readiness Assessment

You ready to step up to leadership, hot shot? The following is a list of competencies you'll need to be effective. Same rules apply: Rate yourself on the same scale of 1 to 5 in each area below (1 = outstanding and 5 = poor), list the specific actions you'll take to earn a perfect score, and compare your assessment to how others rate you.

Leadership Competency	1 (Outstanding)	2	3 (Average)	4	5 (Poor)
Virtues					
Integrity					
Positivity					
Courage					
Commitment					
Continuous Self-Improvement/ Personal Development					
Strategy					
"Big Picture" Planning					
Decision Making					
Innovative/Creative Thinking					

	1 (Outstanding)	2	3 (Average)	4	5 (Poor)
Objective					
Technical					
Technically Sound					
Customer-Focused					
Delegation					
Negotiation					
Interpersonal					
Skilled Communicator					
Accountable					
Trustworthy					
Collaborative					
Empowering					
Professional					
Conflict-Comfortable					
Organizational Savvy					
Influential					

	1 (Outstanding)	2	3 (Average)	4	5 (Poor)
Able to Listen Attentively					
Able to Accept Constructive Feedback					
Generous with Time and Knowledge					
Execution					
Results-Driven					
Time-Wise					
Problem-Solver					
Flexible					
Detail-Oriented					
Networked					
Resourceful					
Able to Manage Risk					

Tool 5: 20 Things Every Career Woman Must Know

1. Lasting success is created by good habits, which are very often destroyed by bad excuses.

2. Hold a grudge and it will hold you back.

3. Goals are short-lived, but virtues are timeless.

4. The most important professional asset you have is your reputation.

5. When you understand there are biological reasons that explain why you act the way you do, you won't feel as crazy.

6. Careers (like diets) don't start tomorrow. Tomorrow's dreams are only achieved by today's action.

7. Sometimes having the right answer is less important than having the right attitude.

8. Not everyone will like you, especially if you have moxie.

9. Authentic outer power comes from authentic inner power.

10. Nice execs finish first. Be kind to people and hard on results.

11. The moment you use sexy to get ahead is the moment you make yourself disposable.

12. The vast majority of decisions affecting your career will happen behind closed doors when you're not in the room.

13. There is a difference between mentors and sponsors. Mentors are concerned with your professional development; sponsors are concerned with your professional achievements.

14. You should always have at least one close contact who has achieved fabulous things beyond your wildest dreams.

15. Chaos is self-created by the choices you are making right now.

16. You'll never criticize yourself powerful, happy, or rich.

17. Confidence isn't having the right answer. It's knowing you can figure out the answer.

18. You will have it all when you don't try to be it all.

19. The secret to productivity is to stop doing things that are comfortable and start doing things that matter.

20. Regardless of your career path, there's no direct flight and the layovers will take longer than you think.

the glass ceiling is only there if you think it is

The theme you choose may change or simply elude you, but being your own story means you can always choose the tone.

—Toni Morrison

A journalist once asked me to describe my "philosophy of success in 20 words or less." While that may be difficult for some people (perhaps downright impossible), I was lucky. My success philosophy has always been under 20 words. Eleven to be exact.

Be your best.

Do your best.

Work hard.

Never give up.

I read those words in a very old book when I was a 14-year-old girl who had no idea what she wanted to do, only that—whatever it was—it had to be big, BIG(!), BIG. Now, two decades later, those 11 words are as true as ever—but the measuring stick has changed. For example, if I asked you to describe a "big" career, you'd probably use words like big pay, big benefits, and big titles. Those are nice, of course, and there's no denying the view is better from the top. (Much better, in fact.) So, yes, that's still the goal.

However—as I've tried to prove to you throughout this book—goals aren't everything. So as you are scaling up your building (whether you're on a ladder or a lattice), don't get so wrapped up in where you're going to be *tomorrow* that you lose sight of where you are *right now*. If you're not sure where you are, ask yourself the following questions:

Am I happy?

Am I respected?

Am I making a difference?

Am I having fun?

Has someone else's behavior changed for the better as a result of my example?

Is my lifestyle comfortable?

If you can honestly answer "yes" to these questions—ta da!—you're successful. As we've already covered, true success isn't what you do, it's *who you are*—and who you are has no ceiling, got it?

Who. You. Are. Has. No. Ceiling.

This is such an incredible, unprecedented time to be a woman in business. Never before has our style of leadership been so needed, and never before have our choices been so vast and our opportunities so great. That said, it's still the *right now* that matters most—not the promise of what's coming around the bend after the next "big" break. *Perhaps you've discovered this already, but if there's one life lesson that still continues to bitch slap us all, it's this: Nothing will work out exactly like you think it will.*

It never does. Maybe, as in my case, you meet the guy who derails your long-planned move to New York City. (Bye-bye to *that* dream!) Maybe you study for years to go into an industry and then one day you realize, *"God, I hate this."* Maybe you have to cut back on your hours because—d'oh!—you're preggers. Whatever life throws at you, if you keep the focus on what you want, you'll never be satisfied. However, if you focus on *who you are*, I promise you'll be better equipped to accept whatever path you're on, even—and perhaps especially—if it doesn't fit the mold of what you had planned.

As I look back on writing this book, I'm reminded that the toughest part of the process has been deciding what to include and what to leave out. There is obviously so much important information that could have been added to every chapter but, frankly, you probably know most of it. I mean, *of course* you need good mentors and sponsors. *Of course* you should wear your name tag on the right. And, yes, odds are good that you could be a stronger, more confident negotiator. For me, the benchmark of this project wasn't necessarily saying important things, but having *something important to say.*

And, as I mentioned in the introduction, there's nothing more important to your success than being a magnificent woman first. Because the truth is, it's not a man's world or a woman's world. It's our world, because it's what we make of it. No ceiling.

And so that's my final wish for you. To work with ease and grace, knowing you're exactly where you need to be and going exactly where you need to go. All you have to do—in this moment—is *be* your best, *do* your best, *work* hard, and *never* give up. Because, trust me, that's the only measuring stick that counts.

index

CPSIA information can be obtained
at www.ICGtesting.com
Printed in the USA
JSHW021946160323
39018JS00006B/69